# MIND, THOUGHT, AYURVEDIC (Plants & Foods) AND YOGA FOR DISEASES

by
SURENDRHANANDA

Order this book online at www.trafford.com
or email orders@trafford.com

Most Trafford titles are also available at major online book retailers.

Note for Librarians: A cataloguing record for this book is available from Library
and Archives Canada at www.collectionscanada.ca/amicus/index-e.html

Printed in Victoria, BC, Canada.

ISBN: 978-1-4269-1308-2

*Our mission is to efficiently provide the world's finest, most comprehensive book publishing
service, enabling every author to experience success. To find out how to publish your book, your
way, and have it available worldwide, visit us online at www.trafford.com*

*Trafford rev. 10/14/09*

 www.trafford.com

**North America & international**
toll-free: 1 888 232 4444 (USA & Canada)
phone: 250 383 6864 ♦ fax: 812 355 4082

# BOOKS BY THE SAME AUTHOR

1. Yoga for individual Practice.

2. The Secret of Pranayama, Relaxation and Concentration.

3. Surya Namaskara "Salutation" for the Children's Life.

4. Reincarnation, Karma (actions) Sex and oneself.

5. Human Body is the Temple of God.

# MIND, THOUGHT
## AYURVEDIC (Plants & Foods)
## AND YOGA FOR DISEASES

Dedicated to all readers and practitioners who follow these Spiritual contents of this Yoga Book.

At the Lotus Feet of Guru (The gateway to Divinity God).

Remember that - PRACTICE MAKES PERFECT IN ONE'S LIFE.

My most humble Pranam at the lotus feet of Guru, Shri Sivananda, Shri Paramhansa Satyananda Saraswati, and Shri Venkatessananda.

The path of Yoga or spirituality is not a withdrawal from the world basic infrastructure or fear; it is learning to be in the world and yet not of the world.

"Remember that no one is alone in this world. He is in everyone and everything. We are ignorant, that's why we ignore Him. Without Him, nothing exists."

SURENDRHANANDA

# Contents

Acknowledgments ............................. xii

Introduction ................................. xiii

Chapter 1 - Discipline of Yoga ...................... 1

Chapter 2 - The Control of the Mind .......... 13

Chapter 3 - Thought ........................... 58

Chapter 4 - Ayurveda or Ayurvedic ............... 76

Chapter 5 - Logic of Ayurvedic Ideology ..... 112

Chapter 6 - Mental Problems ..................... 128

Chapter 7 - Heart Illnesses and High
    Blood Pressure ......................... 142

Chapter 8 - Obesity or Overweight ............. 152

Chapter 9 - Asanas + Pranayamas on
    Spinal Pain and Back Pain ..................... 159

Chapter 10 - Diabetes ................................. 163

Chapter 11 - Eye Problems .......................... 166

Chapter 12 - Conclusion ............................. 171

# A SHORT PRELUDE ABOUT MYSELF

Concerning my educational background, I am neither a well-learned man nor a degree-holder. But with my little English knowledge, I merely want to share my inspirations, experiences and practical experiences of the Science of Yoga to all beings in this material world. I owe greatly my life to the path of Yoga and to my Guru.

I started practising this Royal Path with sincerity and perseverance since my early age. I started the practice because I was having great health problems in general. I did really have great hope in Medical Science (I am not against this medical science) but in my case, I had to take refuge in Yoga. With the help of Swami Venkatessananda of the Divine Life Society at that time, I took to Yoga which was my last resort. Eventually, after a few months of practice of Asanas, Prayanamas, relaxation and concentration, I felt that I was coming back to my original track of normal health. But even then, I was still following my medical treatment and after years, I have recovered fully. Now my spiritual inspirations urge me to write this Yoga book in order to pass and to share the Yoga path and messages to all my fellow-beings of this universe. It needs only Will-Power and Faith to have a little of mind detachment and discrimination with sincere discipline, patience and perseverance to accomplish this truth of Yoga.

However, it is all my inspirations and Spiritual experiences that I am delivering to you all. It is up to you to practise this path of Yoga. As Yoga is an individual practice, no one can do it for you. You need only a Guru or a senior Master. One has not to follow theoretically but to carry on the discipline, practice at a regular time in one's everyday life.

Believe me or not (Sadhana) I mean spiritual practice, patience, perseverance and disciplines are greatly involved throughout the whole life in Yoga. It is really high time for man to awaken himself if he wants a better world for the coming generations. Yoga will definitely help man to alleviate his sufferings and catastrophic situation, mentally and physically.

From my own spiritual point of view, remember well that Man has been given a mind of consciousness to differentiate between the good (God) and the bad (Demon). Unfortunately, Man is involved too much in this illusionary world. And with misconception, ignorance and hypocrisy, Man has taken the unreal body and senses and the world to be the reality, and hence has fallen into the dark net of evils and disillusionment. In fact, this misconception and ignorance and hypocrisy must be turned into the right knowledge of wisdom or God to experience self-realisation as the Self is the sole reality.

However, Man should not only utter a mantra or formula like Aham Brahma, Tat Twam Asi etc, but should positively affirming Him as the only Reality by thought, word and deed. That is if this repentance is done mechanically and theoretically without eradicating the veil of ignorance, this very misconception may inflame the ego.

To end with a little advice from my own spiritual experience. If you find an enlightened Guru, try your level best at least to stick to his guidance and be always at his lotus feet. He is the only one to get you enlightened even if you are in this material world or you are leading an everyday household and conjugal life today. Furthermore, this will greatly help your sons and daughters to follow the good path of Yoga. This is the only way to Godhood or Brotherhood of man and a new spiritual generation to come forward and for a better world in the near future. NO ONE HAS TO RUN AWAY FROM THIS WORLD TO LIVE AS A <u>HERMIT</u>.

N.B. - My only experience:

ADYAPACK - Teacher who teaches languages and Scientific subjects etc.

ACHARYA - He is a scholar and well educated in scriptures and religious books.

GURU - He is the one who has been enlightened himself. So he is the only one gateway to God. That is he is the only Guru to enlighten you in this only life. MY LOVE AND BLESSING BE ALWAYS WITH YOU ALL. PEACE-PEACE-PEACE- OM SHANTI-SHANTI-SHANTI.

"In Spirituality, the death of Ego is the emergency of Divinity".

# ACKNOWLEDGMENTS

I have to thank all those who have helped me heartfully to make this dream a reality. As God does reside in each one of us, we are all in one and one in all.

My special and grateful thanks go to Mr I. Kalloo and family and Mr & Mrs M. K Teeluck for their great assistance, help and supervision in every field work of typing this manuscript in computer as well as the correction which Mr Kalloo has done with all his sincerity. Without his great co-operation, it would have been impossible to realise this book.

I thank heartfully Dr S Vaze (Doctor in Ayurvedic and Master of Yoga) for helping me also in a part of my Yogic life, health and encouraging me to go ahead with this book.

I have also to thank all the family with whom I have resided for years and without their collaboration, it would not also have been possible to write my spiritual inspirations derived from Yoga. They are Mica, Nadhira, Robin, Vimla, Manisha, Eshna and little Girish, Meena, Mewa, little Mehir and Mehak.

And my thanks also go to the printing press and publisher as well.

Finally my thanks go to Mr Ahmad Baboo (my English teacher and writer as well) for his complete revision of this book, without whom it would not have been possible to realize it.

# INTRODUCTION

Yoga is an art of living for the modern era, where many people are suffering from all sorts of diseases, maladies, hectic and stressful living. It is the right time and it's all up to you to decide to start practicing the Yoga path which is being delivered to you. It is also the right time that all your eyes should be opened after learning everyday about the degradation of our beautiful garden, the world. Please don't just read, appreciate and give me credit or praise me for having written all these precious gems about yoga. All these inspirations and experiences should be put into a regular and daily practice and they should become a part and parcel of people's daily living. Many people have made money as their first priority, instead of adoring their inner-self and searching for the truth and reality of themselves within; the greatest quest. and conquest is within.

Nowadays, it is very painful to see people adoring and worshipping the worst thing, which is money in this world, worshipping Mammon. What are we all doing to the precious creation of God? Either we are all forgetting our self or getting and becoming the slave to unreality. We can also witness the downfall of men, how all of them jump in the same bandwagon, and in the same rut of getting married, begetting children and earning money for a decent and luxurious living in this modern life, only to show their ego of name and fame. This is an end without liberation. I am not against this way of life nor do I mean it in a negative way. However, we all have to become one with Him, God, that is from whom we all come. What I mean is that you lead a normal life with simplicity, unity and pure love. It is important that all of you devote about 15 to 30 minutes of your 24hrs to the practice of Yoga within all family and conjugal life; then you will find out the truth for your own self; it will help the new generation to proceed with a sort of spiritual life from the beginning.

To my knowledge, Yoga should be introduced to all family, society, education and in all communities and congregations or clubs and so on. People should be as if infused with this Yogic path and pass it from generation to generation, then there will be a great possibility to change this world from the coming pitfall of savage evolution. And remember it is the word 'involution' rather than 'evolution' which is the most important in human daily life.

However, I am getting the great chance in this human form to share my inspirations and spiritual experience to all the cohabitants of this crucial era. I am here just introducing these thirteen chapters, which I am certain will be of fundamental importance and spiritual help to the fervent and determined practitioners and aspirants.

They are as follows:-

1. Daily disciplines and necessities of Yoga.

2. Mind Control.

3. Thought Control.

4. Ayurvedic

5. Logic of Ayurvedic ideology food

6. Mental problems.

7. Cardio-vascular diseases and high blood pressure

8. Obesity or overweight.

9.  Spinal pains, neck and back pains.

10. Diabetese.

11. Eye problems.

12. Some thoughts

It is now up to the leaders and practitioners to play their own individual role to get out the maximum, to eradicate their maladies or not to be exposed to all sorts of illnesses. It is only by practising them sincerely that the goal will be definitely attained.

According to my spiritual inspiration and experiences, the Yoga path has to be always performed with regular, sincere faith and will-power in order to reach the highest goal in one's life.

However, to my knowledge, even the God, Avatars, Sages, Prophets, Gurus, and Swamis, all of them have performed and practiced the Science of Yoga to reach Godhood in their lives; some after having attained the highest path of Yoga, which means illumination. That is, they must have gone beyond the path of Yoga with sacrifice and purity of love within themselves. So when they have gone to that highest level of God, it is at that stage that common and ordinary material people call them as the above mentioned by spiritual names and meanwhile worship or pray to them because the great majority of ordinary mortals being enmeshed in this material life can't reach these spiritual heights. So now I want to bring to your attention that any individual has this divinity within himself. This divine power is still dormant in most material people, but it can be realized or revealed with Yoga and spiritual practices. Material or common people can't realize this power because they are all entangled in this strong finite material world of diversity and adversity.

It is clear that anyone of you can attain this spiritual goal in whatever religion or community you are following from your birth. You all have got only one biological mother and father who give you birth. They are the real one, either you accept it or not. This is the truth. But with too much involvement in scientific and modern evolution, material people are definitely going out of the real track in their lives and have been plunged in the deterioration of the human condition. We are responsible for this as we are all associated with the savage evolution which is called civilization. But it is a pity to see how all this fast civilization and evolution are going to fall in the darkness of the first creation of the Big Bang, if creation starts from this reality. Actually people should always remain in and practise awareness with sacrifice, purity of love and accept to live in tolerance among all their cohabitants of this planet. But they should not accept or agree blindly to all and everything out of ignorance, as most people are leading their lives with selfish ends and with single mindedness of "Ego-ness" which is haunting this material world.

In fact, true religion is about purity and sacrifice of love. Religion does not involve fanaticism, casteism, fatalist or any dogmatic path to live in this world. People and followers of the major religions do misinterpret these religions, and finally man blindly accepts these bad followers of religions.

For me Religion is LOVE and LOVE is Religion. Remember if you wrongly misinterpret religion as the so-called religious people are doing, then human downfall is not far from getting extinguished together with this changing world. This will be a very sad moment to come. We seem to be accepting to bring the downfall of our children in the coming generation. Either you accept it or not, if humans keep on following these finite and material wrong tracks, more evils will be rampant. It will be a pity to see how, instead of following the good ones, human is off the track and keep on deviating to the bad ones.

It is all due to uncontrollable actions, words, self senses, thoughts and deeds that evils and suffering are prevalent. It is right time that humans learn to realize their spirituality and this will help the whole world to be out of the morass in which it has fallen.

In fact, I am not casting any bad impression or denigrating any religion as I myself am a pure lover of all religions on this earth, which is for me a paradise. After all, they are all one and this one is the great God, the all-pervading one in this whole Universe. Religions have been introduced by the rules and disciplines with the firm pillars of purity of love and sacrifice. It is only the followers that have used religions in the wrong ways and conceptions for their own selfish means and benefits. And eventually they have changed the whole facets of sacrifice and pure love of religion into theoretical routines, rites and ceremonies and dogmas. I do believe and accept all religions as one, but with different paths and I still stay and stick to where I am for I can realize that all is only ONE. Anyway I know it is very difficult to believe and practise this path of truth in this modern world as people have made their mind and thoughts limited and turned the Infinite into finite.

Spirituality can be practised wherever you are and start this search from within yourself, and (know thyself) as the famous Greek spiritual master, SOCRATES, advocated by realizing it.

This highest inner realization as it is called is to go beyond oneself. This is a bit of my own individual's aspiration and experience, which is a rare phenomenon in today's life; Sai Baba is one of those who have realized this. So, when I went to Him to get His Darshan, I had in mind that I was going to see God. But on my first meeting with this phenomenal person. He himself turned to me and pointed out, and exclaimed. "First your Guru only." So I was inspired; it is clear that I have to follow my Guru (Master), who can take me up to the highest i.e to the gate of God. So I have got the right spiritual message from Him.

"Guru Bina Gyanna Nahi."

Without a guru one can't get the real knowledge of wisdom.

Here the reality is that, first try to awake the inner Guru, then the outside Guru will definitely come to your life to guide you to attain what very few others have attained. From my spiritual background, I have found out this reality that the Guru and God are ONE.

Once I was delivering a discourse in a religious congregation; when I ended, a little boy stood up and asked me a question, which was really a very embarrassing one. That question was, "Have you ever seen or known God in your life?"

Suddenly and without any hesitation or any embarrassment, I first replied "He is in form of (Guru) and He is the only ONE with God". And the little boy said that he was satisfied and that is unbelievable.

What I mean here is that, no need to go anywhere; He is within you all, just search for Him internally with practising faith and pure love, sacrifice, detachment of mind, discrimination and finally walk along the only path of the Science of Yoga. The truth will be revealed sooner or later either in this birth or in your next. This self-realization can be realized by any individual but preferably with the guide of an enlightened Guru. Actually there is no alternative way.

Look for spiritual guidance while it is time to awake your innerself whenever and in whatever situation you are. What I mean is that, stay in whatever religion you are and don't convert or divert yourself as the Almighty God is within you all. You have only to reveal Him by switching this light of reality on and within.

Never say that this particular religion is good or that one is bad. This is a sin as all religions have to be followed with pure love and not for selfish ends. Have purity of LOVE within your hearts and practice the control of thoughts, mind and senses of which we are all the prisoners or slaves in this evolutionary and material world. Let your wisdom of knowledge flourish and blossom with the purity of LOVE, sacrifice and the realization of the inner self. Then the next generation will grow up with a positive outlook, then we can call this world a terrestrial paradise, as was the garden of Eden.

These are spiritual clues:-

1. I + material = Hypocrite, ignorant, selfishness (Ego).

2. I + spiritual living = Divinity One with God – That means we are all image of God the Almighty.

3. I – Ego = Soul

4. I + Soul = Divinity – Reach the highest and quality of God as we are all parts and parcels of Him.

5. I + Ego = Material - Hypocrite, Ignorant and Selfish (Ego).

So here I wish all to be as a Lotus flower, which is in water but not touched by water; a natural example on this earth. One must first understand and search for Himself the inner self by treading the path of Reality and Truth in whatever situation.

Nowadays, most people accept God blindly. At present God is unreal because that reality is covered and blinded by the veils of ignorance, hypocrisy and selfishness (Ego). When the removal of these veils of ignorance, hypocrisy and selfishness are done by perfect and regular spiritual practices, then the realization of God is definitely reached.

An example is cited here to open any folded eyes. If it is very dark and you enter a room, you don't see any chair, but when the light is switched on, the chair is visible. The switching of the light within represents the path of Yoga.

The switching on of the light does not create the chair, but only helps to detect the reality which was all the time there in this room, even when it was dark. Therefore, God realization can and need to be a goal. Therefore, understanding of what we are doing means not the understanding of the motive with which we are doing it, but understanding this inner light in which the shadow of motivation is prevented from arising.

Patanjali the creator of Yoga Sastra suggests that "*whatever one is doing, is only a trial to remove the obstructions for the freeflow of consciousness. One should practise Yoga for self purification only. When one purifies oneself, the Truth which exists always, everywhere into oneself is revealed without any difficulty in whatever situation.*"

Therefore, Yoga is not something that can be confined to one day in the week or one hour of the day, but it is to be practised throughout one's living. Here I mean that God dwells in the very core of the heart of everyone, or in the center of these elements earth and space, so that God becomes the reality in all things, animate or inanimate. Watch it carefully as in life the diversity creates a confusion. However, the creator of confusion is the Ego, the "I". One has never cared to examine and analyse it or reflect upon it, because the examiner also becomes this Ego "I". So to erase the Ego "I" from one, the practice must go beyond Yoga and Satwick (Purity) path. The only way in which one can be able to quench his thirst of spirituality is by eliminating this Ego "I" with the following steps:-

1. Attend satsang (be at the lotus feet of Sages, Guru, Swami etc..)

2. Have the miraculous grace of God to be at the lotus feet of Guru and to serve Him with Love.

3. Have discrimination (Viveka) within.

4. Have detachment (vairagya) within.

5.  Read only good spiritual books with sincerity (Swadhya).

6.  Control of mind and thought.

7.  Control over food diet, eat natural food as far as one can.

8.  Control of Breathing system & process (Pranayama).

9.  Practice of Asanas (Postures).

10. Cleanliness of the inner and outside mind, physical and body complex.

11. A good guidance of an enlightened Guru (which is rare in this actual material world. But with determination one will get one definitely).

12. Have faith and will-power in action, word, deed, thought and within oneself.

13. And always think positively in whatever situation one is.

When these above points are attended to and practised perfectly, regularly and sincerely, one then switches off the Ego "I" (which is very strong in this world) and may get enlightment in this very life itself. And I am certain that the past bad karma will be erased and one's life will change from bad to good spiritual path.

Nowadays, in fact, many people complain that they are stressed and suffer many diseases of the hectic life. But if one has a control over the mind, thought, food and breathing process, there will be no room for stress the actual malady of mankind. Stress does not exist; it has been created from within the mind only, when the mind has been weakened.

Vivekananda says:- "*Everything must start from the root. If the root is well formed, organized spiritually, well treated, then there would never have been needed any hospital in this world.*" The large amount of money spent on health development could, however, have been invested and spared into different necessary projects.

I have learnt many things by my own research about the characters of most human beings. Most of their minds are fragmented. Most of them pretend that they are happy and lead a jovial life, but it is all show-off because they are involved too much in money concerns, with family and get themselves stuck 100% in materialistic world and are all are mainly plunged in a rat-race life without an end. Eventually, nearly all of them here become hypocrites, ignorant and selfish (Ego), even those with a highly educated way of life. These people laugh and smile forcibly and externally and will never acquire satisfaction in their lives due to the fierce competition of modern way of living. So stress becomes definitely their master in one way or another. With lots of pressures on their shoulders, they have the guts still to make others believe that they are well-off and live a life full of satisfaction, but this is only on the surface. Really speaking, who can get satisfaction and have pure love and bliss in this junk of material and deceptive world? They are all in the same plight, rich or poor, all are running after a silver coin till death do part them.

It is also a pity to see them wasting their lives in talking and gossiping about others and world affairs. Intellectually, they come to know worldly affairs which are their only interest, but when it comes to know about their own innerself, they are really nowhere. They also show off how much they have learnt and know about material world just to impress others or their adversaries.

But really speaking, they don't know how much they are being fooled by this illusory world. Their desires, envies and pleasures become endless all the way along.

Actually, nothing is yours in this material world, you will have to leave all in whatever circumstances. Only the soul is yours; this body is an instrument and the rest, wives, children, husbands and every relations and objects will disappear. So what one has to do? While living in this human form, one has to realize the innerself while leading a simple living with high thinking spiritually. But I am saddened to find that most people become slaves of this world and in the end with this extraordinary modern hectic lifestyle, they become mentally sick and suffer from many severe diseases and finally they become a burden to somebody's else. With this world of uncertainly, they can't stay still and quiet as their minds become restless and are always occupied and disturbed. They might have a robust and well-built physical body, but for what use if their minds are wavering and there is no mental peace and harmony in this monkey-like mind?

Scientifically, it has been proved that people with restless and sick mental disturbances always create a very negative atmosphere whenever they go in society or get together.

What is the use of living with a robust and strong body if the mind is not at rest, calm and peaceful. That is not called living; that is called existence and lost in this illusory world with only an ordinary life of mating, eating, working, sleeping and enjoying the luxuries of this fake world. I am not against the mundane living, but at least man should realize that he is an image of God, the Almighty. He must use some of this precious time to lift himself spiritually, that is to meditate and perform the unique and infinite Yoga to give him peace of mind and know his innerself; only then, I believe, in this world would there be fewer maladies, physical and mental problems. But if one leads a complete material life style and live interiorly with worries, anger, jealousy, hatred, lust, desires, envy, pride, pleasures and phobia, this way of life leads to ignorance, hypocrisy and selfishness with full of Ego (this world of animal characters) and eventually people become the victims of names and fames, much prevalent in this world of mechanist-materialist pursuits.

Now, I am just giving a clarification about Yoga up to the level of my experiences and inspirations. Yoga really has nothing to do with Hinduism or any other religion. What I mean again here is that Yoga is a Science of its own. Yoga as a science is an art of living and introduces all Asanas (postures) such as Pranamayas (breathing techniques), Mudras, Bandhas etc., for the welfare of this human body and mind complex. The above mentioned exercises have been created from the law of nature and we are all parts and parcels of this infinite universe and the infinite nature as well. They are all the movements, exercises, postures and breathing system, which are related logically to the five elements, plants of all kinds, birds, fishes, animals etc. Remember that without nature, no human would have been able to survive on this planet. I am convinced of one thing: we have other planets in different universe which are inhabited by other human beings who are more developed and much more advanced compared with us on this planet Earth. This can be found only if one goes beyond the highest level of meditation and path of yoga. This is a true fact because this mind is really infinite as well; if one can go into the outer infinity then this is possible to believe.

However, everyone must follow his religion firmly with pure LOVE. Do not follow religion as to become mere fanatics or misguided cranks. In no religion has there been any dirty such thing as fanaticism and intolerance. You must all practise LOVE as this is the main principle of religion to each of us. If the religion of pure LOVE is ingrained in each individual deeply, then all humanity can live and make this world like multi-coloured roses in a beautiful garden. Imagine how beautiful and vivid this garden will appear to each of us, where there will be only peace and harmony among all races, colours and religions. If each of us sees only that humanity within all of us and the oneness within, then it is probable that no religion, race or creed will make any difference in this world which is all ours. We will all live in a freedom world with this pure Love spreading all over our own individuality. This world can be made as a Terrestrial Paradise with characters of Pure and love within each individual.

There can never be only one religion to rule the whole humanity. But there can be only one race of humanity with always many groups of religions and sects as these are the cause and effect of the Law of nature. As there is only one soul which is in every body but not many souls as some imagine.

Now, this is an image of myself. As I have mentioned I don't want to fall in the same rut as most human beings are doing in this evolving material world. I am born to make my own experience. I am not imposing on any one to follow me as we are all free in this world to follow whatever trend of life one wants. But my experience is to stay in this world and don't let the world be within me. Use the minimum of this material world while following an enlightened Guru through whom one can attain one's spiritual goal.

However, this should not be interpreted as showing you my Ego which you might speculate, but my truth about my own visualization, inspirations and practice of life. Most people might question my way of living and how I am leading such a life without earning a living in that modern world and what is my aim in this world, whether this life is meant for others, as one should go deeply within to discover about the past, present and future karma. It would be possible if someone does this and it all depends on the Law of Karma.

Frankly the answer is very easy and true to realize. I am trying to attain the path of Yoga and find out if I am really the image of God : even living in this modern world, I realize that I am the microcosm of the macrocosm. First of all, I am following certain disciplines, that is to detach my mind from wealth, women and wine, which have not such importance in my way of spiritual living. These are the 3 important factors that prevail in the world. So to lead an illusionary life, people are bound to get trapped in this vicious circle because they have made it an important rule and without these three cravings, there would be no life worth living to them in this world. It is true materially, if one wants to live for further production of human beings. So this life is only temporary where there are happiness and sorrow only. One comes in crying and leaves this world either dying with diseases, or with a premature death crying again. That is the cycle of birth and death. People don't have time to think how to leave this world, with a spiritual conception of becoming immortal. Once, a sage remarked at the birth of a babe: "You are coming in this world crying while everybody is smiling around you; live in such a way that when you die, you smile and are happy while everybody around is weeping."

Anyway I know I am born in this world to search for my own reality and truth to get bliss within, in whatever circumstances and to realize my immortality and soul. This is my spiritual aim in my life in this world of sorrow and happiness.

If Jesus has proved that He and His father are ONE, so I also can realize this because as He encased in a human body by practicing spiritual disciplines, He realized this. If he had these qualities within, that proves that all human beings have these qualities, but unfortunately they are sleeping within. Jesus has said, "The Kingdom of God is within you." We have to implode these the spiritual secrets which are within all of us, either you believe me or not. By real trial, one can come to this realization about this path of perfect-ness in this only human form. But if you let spiritual world dormant within you, it is because the real obstacles are like a wall in your life of today.

Actually this world could have become again a kingdom of God, if people start again to divert their characters to wisdom of knowledge and by practicing from childhood the real paths of spirituality and the Science of Yoga. But it is a pity and sad to see how most people live as lions within the lamb's skin. What I mean here is that people are full of hypocrisy, ignorance and selfishness (Ego) which shape them into horrible and monstrous characters. These are the three first enemies for human beings' downfall. Believe me, most people have built up within themselves these horrible traits nowadays. That is why this world is fast approaching a terrestrial disaster and hell. One more thing which is very dangerous is that the scientists are going too far and even beyond their limits and this could bring a deterioration of the complete atmospheric system of our planet, Earth. One day life itself would completely disappear just like what happened to planet Mars where life existed millions and millions years ago. That does not mean that I am against the scientists but they should remain according to their limit and don't by-pass God's work.

May I pray God the Almighty to help humans to be out of this coming catastrophic and critical situation. This catastrophic event will all be man's outcome if he does not use his mind properly. It is high time that people start realizing spiritually, so that the coming generation may be safe and protected. If not, we humans will be extinct from our own world similarly to what happened to those ancient giant animals like the dinosaurs.

However, I am born to experience and inspire my Innerself which is the truth and don't want to follow or repeat the same mistakes like my fore-fathers and parents. I don't want to run in the same rut as they have done; after all, I am born out of my own past Karma, and if one binds oneself to karmic Law, one will understand what I mean here and come out of this enslaving and imprisoned life in this material world.

Unfortunately, this is not meant for everybody. I have come on this terrestrial Paradise in a human form. Maybe after so many thousands or millions of years born in many species and now very fortunate to be in this rare special form of a human! Why then let myself be retrograded again to these lower species? So here, I have to find out and search for my real root and source inorder to return to

Him, the Fatherhood or Godhood, which is the highest destination within human life. That is to liberate and not to entangle oneself in this vicious circle of birth and death. And believe me, this life is a rare gift and we the only species in which one gets the fortunate occasion to be liberated and go to Him, the divinity God.

Now after having witnessed all these sufferings of humanity on this world planet, I am just giving the solutions about the path of Yoga and spirituality which is the inner realization to remedy and alleviate all these sufferings and to restore them and show them the only right road to the Divinity within themselves. Truly speaking, we are all image of God. By fulfilling and following these simple disciplines, postures and Pranayama of yoga in one's daily life, people will be able to know the truth by themselves.

Actually most of the cohabitants of this earth lead the same routine of material living, with a conjugal life with children, working, earning money, sleeping, mating, drinking, eating and enjoying the pleasures and desires of this material world pursuits which end here itself. At least try to spare some few minutes daily to try to know the reality within, that is their own innerself; this is achieved by meditation, alone in a quiet place.

From my point of view, nothing is impossible; if one has faith, willpower, detachment of mind, discrimination, discipline, pure love, sacrifice and devotion, then this definitely become possible and easy. But this depends on one's past Karma as well and it is not meant for everyone to do it. Anyway, I believe that our destiny is within our own hands. This world is full of ups and downs, happiness and sorrow. But one must live a life as the salmon fish always swimming against the opposite tide and current in the river.

What I mean is that one has to face all sorts of difficulties but face them with full faith, positive attitude, will-power, detachment, discrimination, and with pure love and sacrifice within one's inner-self. If one builds up a very strong mind with pure and good thoughts, deeds, words, actions and with the help of an enlightened Guru (spiritual master), one will definitely attain this path of liberation in this rare human life form. If one faces all these adversities with equanimity with God love, with inner-self faith and with the above-mentioned spiritual activities, one is really the king of kings in this only life. So when one reaches the highest spiritual level, one can find nothing hard in this life whatever the circumstances. One becomes fully non-attached to all material objects in this life. At that spiritual level, one can see only Him interiorly and exteriorly. One gets himself liberated mentally, physically, thoughtfully and consciously. One becomes really a free soul. At that level, nothing can affect a liberated character. He becomes as the lotus flower of which you all know. It is not easy to get up to that level as I have said; only a handful of well trained spiritual beings can reach it. But it is possible.

*May Guru'grace help humanity*

*To be awakened within this only*

*Human form to the image of God*

N.B. 1. Yogic type of life 2. Ordinary Student to stay far from disease

Many people imagine that a Yogi is a starved and haggard man, a skin and bone specimen; they are wrong. A Yogi takes much care of his body and mind complex. The Yogi never eats any meat or improper food. He keeps his system pure in order to pursue advanced practices which make the body too sensitive for coarse food. He undergoes this training and discipline and has to keep to a very strict diet.

2. But a student who does Yoga exercises for the improvement of his health only does not have to keep any special diet if he doesn't want to and he can eat as he pleases with little disciplines to avoid all these modern pathological material life. (But he should not gulp down the food as actually he does in a hurry. He should masticate slowly and let the food rise with the saliva to help the stomach from forcing the digestion).

Two points to be noted here:

1. One might have a frail skeleton and body, but if one's mind is pure, calm and strong with a complete awareness, one can realize the self and reach the road to perfection in this human form and within this material world itself.

2. One might have a strong and healthy body, but if the mind is weak and can't control it, one becomes ignorant and gets entangled in the five senses and the Ego; that man becomes a slave to his desires, envy etc. What's the use of living as a dead corpse!

It is high time to take a good and spiritual decision to save our world for the coming generation. The real education starts from the new couple life and the children from their mother's womb, and from their home and the way of living in their house.

I wish that there are no names for God, as He is limitless and infinite. But it is a pity to see so called religious people giving names to God in each religion and turning Him to be limited and finite; instead I prefer people to practise the Yoga of Love and see Him within themselves. Then one can reach the infinite and see Him in everything, animate or inanimate . Of course, practice is greatly needed, not only in theory.

N.B: Remember that I have written a special chapter on Ayurvedic i.e, a few natural plants, leaves that are really very helpful to the human body inorder to keep it fit and healthy. They might be expensive but they are of great value to the human body and mind in general. Personally, I have made and done this experience. The practice is done and then I pass it on to others for their healthy benefits.

Finally, a brief writing is done on Ayurvedic as the daily food consuming for our health benefits. They are the vegetables which nearly everyone consumes in the food to build up the body and mind complex; without food no one can survive

"You are what you eat"

We very often, however, dig our graves with our teeth.

# CHAPTER 1

# DISCIPLINE OF YOGA

"One ounce of practice is better than tons of theory" "True spirituality goes beyond all religions." "Spiritual discipline is the highest action that one can do to himself and to raise his innerself to Godhead. Remember that in your entire life span, you can change only one person and that is yourself." Daily disciplines and necessities are of great advantages in practising Yogic Postures. So if Yoga is done irregularly and without good preparation, the body and mind complex will not grow to the full benefit. A regular daily habit or routine will be of great advantage as encapsulated in the above quotes.

It has been proved that in Yoga research that diseases, disorders and ailments are the outcome of wrong ways of leading one's daily living, of bad habits, of lack of proper knowledge of things related to the individual's way of life and wrong food. When there is the malfunctioning of the body, diseases start to infest the body and mind complex. So due to certain weaknesses and wrong notions of the individuals, the malfunctioning is awakened by the interior imbalance in the body and mind complex. The cause of the disease and cure in both cases depends upon the individual himself.

In order to understand Yoga properly, 6 important things are needed:-

1. Control of the mind and thoughts.

2. Food balance.

3. Breathing system.

4. Developing the regular and daily practice of Yoga.

5. Relaxation.

6. Concentration.

Actually the necessities of Yoga practice are.

To gain full benefit of Yoga it is important to understand some principles and instructions connected to Yoga practice:-

Timing:- Early morning time is the best time for practising Yoga, but one can practise it in the evening as well or at any other time convenient, provided the stomach is empty and not heavy with food. Remember that there should be an interval of 3 to 4 hours after eating, before performing Yoga. And a gap of half an hour should be given after drinking any liquid.

Yoga should be practised regularly at the same time everyday for at least five to six days in a week which would be enough to get benefit. One must get up early in the morning. Early to sleep and early to rise is a maxim no where more appropriate as here. Sleep early brings sound sleep, makes the mind calm and the thoughts pure. Early waking up removes laziness and brings agility in the body and the mind. One who gets up early is able to finish with his daily chores like walking, exercise and cleaning bowels without undue haste. One should go as well for bowel evacuation at a fixed time every morning. The very first condition for perfect health is the daily cleaning of the bowels regularly as well as practically. This will make one's body light and increase one's appetite.

Brushing the teeth:- One must clean one's teeth in the morning, but remember that cleaning them before going to bed is the most important one, for the food particles left in the teeth rot in the mouth during the night and this helps to decay the teeth, and the gums become very sensible. The chewing is an exercise to the teeth. One must chew one's food properly and this also helps to facilitate the task of the digestive system.

Bathing :- One can take a bath either before or after Yoga exercise, no general rule is applied. It is very essential to take a daily morning bath with fresh water mainly after exercises. This also helps to keep the skin clean and pores of the skin to open. One should take a bath as an art. One should rub or massage one's body gently inorder to produce some body heat before taking a fresh bath. The advantage of bathing with fresh water is that it helps to bring the blood circulation up to the skin. It also imparts activeness and freshness to the body and mind.

Clothes:- Simple and comfortable clothes should be used. The clothes should be loose, suitable and should be of cotton material.

Place:- Always practise Yoga on the floor, use a carpet, rug or mat on the floor. The place of practice should be neat, clean and well ventilated. During winter, draft of cold wind should be avoided. If possible avoid air condition.

Silence:- One should keep silence while performing Yoga practices. Avoid any conversation, mental activity and even listening to music. So silence helps in preserving energy as well as in being attentive during Yoga practice.

Rest:- Bear in mind that there are two sorts of rest in Yoga:

1. Short rest:- This short rest should be for sixth or eight seconds only and it is taken between one and other asana. The short rest is completed by breathing twice at the completion of one round of a posture or asana.

2. The long rest:- This is done at the end of all the asanas, pranayamas and other kriyas which one does at a stretch. An example here if one does Yoga for twenty minutes, the rest (shavasana dead corpse) at the end should be for five to ten minutes.

Dress:- When doing Yoga a minimum of clothes should be on the body. A male practitioner can wear half pant or pijamas along with an underwear. Ladies can wear either slacks or stretch pants with blouse. And in winter, light wollen clothes may be worn while practising Yoga.

Method of practising:- To get the real benefit of Yoga one must practise yoga in a disciplined way. Yoga is a scientific system; it needs to be performed in a methodical and specifies manner. If not, it becomes only an exercise and will not bring any satisfactory results. Yoga should be done according to the limits of one's body. Do it as much as one can. One need not be in a perfect form. If one cannot do the full posture, do half of it or even less. One should perform all the steps carefully and very slowly. Start to practice with only a few postures in the first week, and then add two more postures during the second week. And in this manner every week new postures can be added according to the requirement and recommendation. One thing, if it is possible to follow a Master's advice, this will be better.

Female precautions:- Female practitioners should avoid Yoga practice during menstrual period and during advanced level after the fourth month of pregnancy. After the fourth month, pregnant women have to practice Yoga on a selection basis under the proper care and instruction of a Master. Proper practice of Yoga during early stage pregnancy enhances the health of the baby in the womb and it helps also to make the delivery painless.

Duration of Practicing Yoga:- In winter season, one can practise longer time than in summer time. Maximum time devoted to practising Yoga should not exceed forty five minutes in a single day of winter for the common people. During summer time, maximum practice should be thirty minutes.

Only one session of Yoga practice is enough in a day, but those who feel like doing it the evening can still perform it. Finally a minimum practice of fifteen to twenty minutes per day is quite reasonable for the common man to maintain good health.

Behaviour of a good practitioner:- Yoga is meaningless if there is no obvious change in the social behaviour of the practitioner. A Yoga disciple should always think good of others. He must not be greedy and selfish. He must lead a simple life, as "simplicity is divinity." Such a life should be without causing, or even without desiring to cause harm to anyone. He is sweet to others and always wants to stay among good companions. He should avoid to be among dissolute and materialistic characters. This will help him to become very strong, mainly with a complete control of mind, viveka (discrimination) and vairagya/detachment). He must like to serve others in whatever situation. Finally all these bring him nearer to his goal i.e the Vairagya highest or union with Almighty (God).

Balanced Diet:- A proper understanding of some of the principles and advice about food would help the practitioners to realize the importance of food and its effects on the body system in a clear way.

Food is a dominant part in the system of Yoga. It is also mentioned that you are what you eat. However, the kind and quality of food affect the body and mind complex of the individual. The individual who does not eat a balanced and proper food, and who does not have a clear understanding of the disciplines of eating, often starts to damage his own body and mind complex. Finally one starts to feel the bad effects of an improper dietary habits on his behaviour, appearance, thoughts, speech and actions as well. However, the individual whose appearance, thoughts, actions manifest undesirable consequences would justify the dictum: "You are what you eat."

Here Yoga applies to three types of food and the effects on the human body and mind complex. They are Rajasic, Tamasic and Satwic.

1. Rajasic food:-

In fact Rajasic food includes a variety of delicious dishes in any community or race. Naturally the dishes are being prepared of various kinds:- some fried, some roasted, and some curries highly seasoned and in the end together with various sweets and drinks would be offered. So foods of this variety are considered undesirable for those who practise Yoga as they create extra weight, fat and generate feeling of heaviness for a longer period of time after dinner, the passions are also aroused.

Tamasic food:- This type of food is prepared with hot stuff. These foods are being used with too much spices and with excessive uses of salts, pepper, chilli and similar other seasonings in either vegetarian or non-vegetarian. Finally these types of food are suitable to those who have a coarse nature, a rough temperament, and are inclined to be noisy, quarrelsome and intolerant. So these are not advisable for a practitioner of Yoga.

Satwic food:- This type of food is being prepared with moderation and the mind should be pure while preparing the food. The food when prepared requires less amount of spices and seasoning are being used. The food should be fresh, attractive and nutritious and is cooked as well in simple and divine way. And this one is recommended for those who practise Yoga on large scale in their daily life.

This is to be noted that no food neither vegetarian nor non-vegetarian is by itself rajasic, tamasic and satwic. The importance here is that the method of preparation and not the food itself. There is a wrong thinking that the non-vegetarian food is tamasic and the vegetarian food is satwic, remember that potato and cauliflower can be prepared as tamasic and meat, chicken or fish can be cooked as satwick, depending upon the choice of the individual, physically and mentally.

Now it is the quality and its preparation that is considered. Many have a wrong idea that by reducing their eating of food or reducing the calories, they would lose extra weight. And otherwise many feel that perhaps by eating heavily, they would get more weight, such wrong thinking is really undesirable, as both these extremes have a harmful effect on the individual. Either a man is overweight or underweight, the Yogic disciples and methods of eating remain unchangeable.

As the food is being divided into three types, the mind as well depends upon its qualities such as :- Satwick Mind, Rajastic Mind and Tamasic Mind.

1. Satwick Mind:- Satwick Mind remains under complete peace and stays cool like the moon on the full moon night. Here the characteristics of the mind are kindness, truth, contentment,

love, devotion, humanity, happiness, tolerance and forgiveness etc... This is to remind you that in this situation, the blood pressure remains normal and the living cells multiply and become stronger. This sort of man endowed with this type of mind can control and develop his body as well.

2. Rajasic Mind:- This state of mind is overshadowed by the cleverness of the intellect. The mind then stumbles in the darkness of worry, sorrow, jealousy, greed, anger, fear and luxury. In this condition, the blood circulation becomes abnormally rapid and this takes to disturbance and confusion in the body. The cells also get into disturbing state. So with disturbance of growth and development, the cells get disorganized and deteriorated and this brings weakness. And finally the body health is bound to suffer as well.

3. Tamasic Mind:- People in this state are ignorant and wild. This leads to theft, deceit, ignorance, laziness, violence, adultery and other sinful activities; so, when one is contaminated with these worst impulses, life also gets deteriorated. If one starts taking pleasure in all these lower activities, the thinking is completely confused, because the blood circulation also gets disorganized and here as well the cells stop to work normally. In this situation, the cells get filled with poisonous instead of vigorous ones. And it is sure that no one can save a man from this downfall.

However, mental health is the first requisite not only for the growth and development of this mind, but for the whole body as well. So it is better to have and practise a Satwick mental quality through regular effort and faith. Therefore bear in mind that mental and physical health is indivisible and dependent on each other. If the mind is ill and perturbed, it is impossible for the living cells to become strong and to get growing. On the other hand, if the body is ill, it will make the mind confused and helpless, as it won't be able to control and guide the body functions.

Discipline of food:- The Yogic discipline of eating good food: first a balanced diet is the most important discipline of the daily life. A balanced diet includes four items: salad, fresh vegetables, fresh fruit and raw nuts. They should cover the major dishes of the day.

Salads:- All the raw vegetables which one eats constitute salads. They are cucumber, tomatoes, carrots, lettuce, cauliflower, cabbage. These should be prepared by cutting them into pieces and with a little dressing, and can be eaten raw in the quantity of about a little bowl everyday and they should be eaten before lunch or dinner.

Fresh Veg: Vegetables should be fresh. The vegetable must not be dried and deformed. Fresh vegetables should be consumed into proportionate quantity in one's daily life. They also should be prepared in a satvick method.

Fruit Fresh Only:- Fruits are very nutritious food for the individual in daily life. Every day the fresh fruits are essential. Any fruits that are easily available would even be very useful for the purpose. All fruits have nearly all nutritious value, whether they are cheap or expensive. They can be taken single or mixed with various types. Remember that there are fruits which are seasonal. An individual can eat two or three fruits daily. He may take a banana, guavas, oranges, apples or etc etc. The most important point is that fruits should be consumed on a daily basis to get a better health.

Nuts mainly raw:- Nuts such as cashew, pistachio, almond, walnuts, pecans, etc must be taken out from hard shells and this type of nuts is very much recommended to be eaten daily. A handful of these nuts would be enough daily. As these nuts have a warm effect on the body, they are recommended to be more consumed in winter and a little consumption during summer. These nuts are full of proteins, minerals and vitamins. And taken in a proper way they help to energize and give health to the body .

Other disciplines :- Now besides the balanced diet, there are other disciplines to be followed to get good results. First thing is the method of eating the food. The food should be eaten very slowly and swallowed thoroughly by crushing and chewing. Nowadays most people, just eat the food too fast due to lack of time in their daily hectic life. People have developed the bad habit of fast eaters. Maybe to them, chewing and then swallowing is perhaps boring and enjoyable. Fast eating has very ill effects on the digestive system as a whole. Much emphasis is laid on slow eating as it is more important. For example, one can eat a banana much faster than an apple or fish than meat. But the most fundamental importance is that the food must be chewed till it is rolled up and then swallowed.

The most important thing is that the saliva should be properly mixed up with the food to make it easy to digest. The slow eater gets whole benefits and meanwhile gets full satisfaction in dinner or lunch even when he eats only a little amount of food. His body gets the time to absorb the full use of any food eaten, and he maintains a better health by even taking less quantity of food.

One should eat only about 85% of his capacity, and the stomach should have a little space left after dinner or lunch for the circulation of wind. The intakes become easy to digest and the body can make full use of it. By eating more than the capacity, the individual is actually over straining the abdominal, digestive system of the body in general; the physical performance and the mental powers are being also disturbed. Finally overeating naturally puts extra and unnecessary weight.

Now about the eating habits, man should eat only four times within twenty four hours. He should eat at least two hours before going to bed. One must have breakfast in the morning, lunch at noon, some refreshment during afternoon and dinner in the early evening. Remember that eating four times should be made a daily habit.

The water drinking must be taken into great consideration. It is advisable to drink at least ten to twelve glasses daily. It is a very bad habit to drink water while eating. Water should be drunk ½ an hour before or after eating. Remember that by drinking plenty of water, this helps to keep out impurities of the system.

Here it is highly recommended that alcoholic drinks and spices should be taken with much moderation if taken in one's daily life; but it is advisable to avoid them if possible, if one wants to have a healthy body and mind complex.

Spices such as salt, chilli, pepper and other herbs should be used at a minimum when foods are prepared. It is not meant that spices are bad, but they must be used at a minimum. The seasoning as well can be done for flavour, but excessive use should also be avoided.

Coffee and Tea also are injurious to health. They should be taken in moderation not in excess as modern people are consuming. Two cups are enough within twenty four hours. Both these drinks cause constipation, insomnia, nervous tension and distort the natural complexion of skin. In excess they are an harassment to the body and brain.

Alcoholic drinks are intoxicative and weaken the individual, physically and mentally, if drinks without restraint or control. And if a daily habit of drinking is continued, it would be very harmful to the body. Do avoid making a habit to kill innocently the body and brain complex ignorantly.

N.B Gram (chickpeas) soaked and sprouted grain is very much recommended, it is a highly nutritious grain. It is as well full of protein, mineral and vitamins. An often intake of a handful of germinated gram is very inducive to good health . Gram should be soak in water for about eight hours and eat them in the early morning.

The diet or food is really so simple and if these above principles are followed and make a habit of eating with discipline, one is certain to maintain excellent health. Furthermore, if a balanced diet along with proper hygienic system and care is taken with regular practice of Yoga, one would definitely be guaranteed of developing and keeping a proportionate figure and dynamic health.

Now not to go deep in these, the hygienic care involves proper bath and cleaning daily habits which all of you know about. Bath, rubbing, body cleaning shampooing, hair precaution, teeth, a bit of oil massage if possible. These basic daily formalities are done by every one in his daily life from morning to evening. So I don't have much to say on these cleansing of daily life.

Before ending this chapter, I would like to advise everybody to please follow the practice of some simple Yoga postures, Prayanamas, relaxation, concentration and finally a heartfully and sincere repetition with love of God in one's daily morning, plus all the above disciplines about the advice of food. One will definitely reach a high goal even in this evolution of modern life.

Remember (simplicity is Divinity). May thy Lord bless you all, to keep this body healthy which is a Temple of God.

# CHAPTER 2

# THE CONTROL OF THE MIND

*"If someone has no control over his mind and thoughts, he cannot have peace of mind. And if one has no peace of mind, how can he have happiness? If one is a victim of passions, emotions and tension, he may develop obstinate mental maladies. It is said that a man may have received the grace and blessing of God, of the teacher and of holy men, but if he does not have the grace of his own control of the mind and thought, he will go to ruin. Having this grace of one's own mind also means having full control of it.*

*With the highest positive and control of mind and thought, one can attain spiritual illumination. A controlled mind can easily be concentrated and through concentration of mind one can gain knowledge and knowledge is power. A controlled state of mind leads to calmness and calmness leads to peace of mind and peace of mind leads to happiness "Bliss". Therefore a happy man makes others happy.*

*Finally a man of controlled mind will be free from mental maladies and physical ailments caused by mental tension."*

"Human beings of this world are living in complete material turmoil and whirlpool. Spirituality is the only resort to help humans to get out of this distressful situation. If not the degradation of this world will be worse and worse. Sooner or later the end of this world is approaching as the death of planet Mars happened long time ago."

"The vital part of all Yoga and Spiritual knowledge is the control of mind. Mind control is the key not only for climbing the ladder of the spiritual expansion in life, but also for achieving success gradually in the practical life. With this success of controlling the mind, peace, happiness and bliss rise naturally. If one studies also the law of nature, one will definitely understand the natural law of the daily life." The above citations are helpful in life.

Actually all the pains, sufferings and miseries of the modern era are due to not having a proper control of the mind. Most people instead of developing a mastery of their mind, have become its slave. Once they become slave of mental restlessness, they run from here to there according to its caprice. So they go in different and irrelevant directions of their life with many misguidings and failures of life. As they say, money is not only everything. The servant gets mastery over the master if he believes in money but vice versa if he is spiritual. In order to control the mind, the master has to keep his real mastery status and put the servant in his actual place. If a spiritual student wants to be truly cheerful, happy and peaceful in this life, he must be able to control and fix his mind where he wants really to keep it and prevent it from wavering form one place to another.

Unless the control of mind is done and overcome with faithfulness and sincerity, one is bound to be unhappy and get stressed. This is the worst disease of this era. It is difficult to avoid it because of the pressures of this modern life, where time is limited in everyone's life. Too many things are being done feverishly, where there is an acquisitive and competitive way in every field of activity. It is all due to the hectic pace of this modern living, the "Tofflan Future Shock." What makes one different form each other is the capability of controlling the mind.

A mind which is restless vacillates constantly from thought to another thought; it does not stay fixed or stable for any second or minute. It is very clear as one thought goes, another replaces the other thought and imagine how can this chain of thought ever end. Remember how this restless mind never let you at peace, even in your precious sleep; you still have dreams, nightmares. This restless mind is always alert in any situation, good or crucial at all time. The more one tries to control it, the more vicious it throws one back up and makes one more unstable, agitated and more confused with distressful problems.

However, there are several feelings and emotions such as likes, dislikes, love and hatred, envy, greed, anger, revenge, jealously, fear, pride, worries, anxieties, regretful attachments - all these emotions and feelings are originated mentally because of the inability of the mind to face life or the material world as it should be. The uncontrolled mind gets contaminated by the dualities of every day life 1. success and failure, 2. gain and loss, 3. life and death, 4. pleasure and pain, 5. union and separation and so on, from which the distinct mind is excited and thrilled over one time, while it is greatly frustrated, tense and depressed in other time. If one wants to become a complete transformed character with a constant peaceful and cheerful attitude, one must vanquish one's mental agitation and bring it under control. Nothing and nobody on earth and in whatever situation can deviate from one's circumstance of equilibrium. On reaching the highest state of mind control, all external circumstances lose grip over the practitioner and succumb themselves at his lotus feet. One can act as a rock amidst all negative situations with will, one can have the power to move the whole world and become the king of the kings as it is said. If one acquires a character in life, one is very fortunate because such a man is a source of light and divine power. There is an example; the power of a man who has complete control of his mind definitely pushes up manifold in the same way as the power of running water elevates when it is being controlled by building or erecting a dam.

To conquer the mind, although difficult, yet with complete sincerity, constant practice and firm determination, it can be possible. It is indeed a long life practice with perseverance and the rewards are eventually worthwhile.

Remember that before starting the practice of controlling the mind, the practitioner must have a complete understanding of the basic nature and characteristic of the mind. Bear in mind that without understanding the mind's basic nature and characteristic, it might lead to nowhere and failure. Here any attempt is of fundamental importance to control the mind. You might read or hear people complain of not being able to control the mind, despite long years of practice, due to neglect of the first essential, that is the understanding of its basic nature and characteristic.

Before going further, a brief idea of the basic nature and characteristic is elucidated to the practitioner:

Mind and its nature

1. Know your mind.

2. Brain is part of body instrument.

3. mind is soul

4. Mind can't see. Brain can see with the physical ego.

5. Mind is immortal just like soul.

6. Nature of mind is indivisible.

7. Mind is self emerged and self luminous.

8. Body depends upon the mind.

9.  Where mind is situated in the body.

10. Finally influence of mind and body depends on each other.

Before going into the basic nature and characteristic of the mind, let me give you a reasonably clear explanation and understanding of the mind throughout the meditational practices, as adopted by a modern psychological division of the mind.

The mind is divided into four principal parts:

1.  The lower or instructive.

2.  the rational.

3.  the illuminative and.

4.  the collective unconscious (cosmic mind).

1.  The lower mind:- Actually this part of the mind deals with co-ordination and activation of the different sections of the organs of the body. It operates the systems of respiration, circulation, digestion and other processes in the body. It acts as a device like as a computer which ensures or protects the different parts of the body to work harmoniously in order that the body performs as a co-ordinating item.

    It is also the cause of our instinctive impulses such as thirst, hunger, procreation, self-preservation and other main controls.

    Remember that these instincts are very often powerful and overcome the rest of the mind. It is really this part of the mind which is the cause of the complexes, phobias, conflicts and other mental problems that make life miserable. Generally these obsessions are charged with intense emotions. After all, it is a storehouse of the compulsions that stimulate most of the actions.

2. The rational mind:- This is the second part of the mind which works principally during the waking state. And this part is mostly accessible to awareness. It is after all the lake of rational thinking, for it is here that datas are accumulated from everyday experience in life. It is where the incoming data is examined and compared with the previous memories, so that the logic deduction or thoughts arise to conscious perception.

Really speaking, the very thoughts that are thinking right now spring from this only section of the mind. It is the problem-solving region of the mind, which gives the answers as required. Very often most of this problem-solving occurs without our awareness.

An example (many people have had a querry which defies answers at a certain time, yet without their knowing it, the problem is being faced in the rational part of the mind, so that at a later time the answer suddenly dashes to the conscious perception or one tries to recall somebody's name and cannot, then suddenly it appears at a later time. Finally this is the task of the rational or logical mind).

3. The illuminative mind:- This is oftenly said to be the region of super-consciousness or people of genius quality. It is this region of the mind which receives instinct, flashes or inspirations. Without this section of the mind, the great intellectuals or artists or poets would not have been able to create their mysteries, masterpieces or scientists to receive insight into the phenomena of this Universe. Remember also that it is from this

part that great Saints and Yogis derive their revelations, deeper knowledge, wisdom, bliss and transcendental experiences.

Actually, in this illusive material world, very few people are acquainted with this illuminative mind. Most people tend to be imprisoned by the links of the rational lower mind. Finally, it is sad to say that this region of illuminative mind has been wholly neglected by psychologists in the past. It is only recently that there has been a wide interest in this field, especially from the works of C. Jung.

4.  The collective unconscious mind:- It is this part of the mind which contains a whole record of the evolutionary past, brought to light by psychologists. It is a region of unbelievable and immeasurable fathom that contains the information and activities of the past ancestral life. It is a lake of archetypes that has accumulated or perhaps guided over the period of millions of years, though it could say that it is beyond definition in terms of time. People think it is the inner equivalent to the story of creation and the universe.

Actually, it is an infinite blue print of the inner and outer Cosmos. And this infinite links all of us together.

First the lower and rational aspects of mind contain the characteristics that elaborate the individual personality. Secondly, the illuminative mind (Super Conscious) and collective unconscious regions are on other hand, supra personal (beyond the personality). That is, they transcend individuality and are common ground of all of the people.

Actually, the superconscious division can probably be regarded as an integral part of the collective unconscious, but they have been divided for convenience of description. The superconscious region is that part of the collective unconscious from which one gets most sublime illuminations. The rest of the collective unconscious contains the accumulated experience of existence, that which is beautiful and that which is ugly, that which seems relevant and that which seems irrelevant to one's life. The collective unconscious mind is really neutral in its nature. It is in a sense everywhere, under, above, within and without. It transcends the individualized mind.

Anyway, it is when people reach that highest stage that they can believe in this. It is impossible to believe it when people live in the lower and rational mind. It is a question of practice in Yoga with discipline in the controlling of the monkey mind, that is greatly counted here.

Most of us spend our lives totally extroverted, failing to realize that an ocean of bliss and knowledge exists within each of us, merely waiting to be tapped and discovered. It is always there and we are always in contact with these deeper aspects, but we don't know it. Our level of awareness is insufficient. The method to be aware and know this intimate link is of course meditation leading to the inner conquest.

The basic characteristics of the mind:- Man has got such a gift by virtue of possessing a mind by which he is able to be conscious and aware of himself. He also has consciousness and awareness of self and others which are the basic nature of mind. With this mind he can distinguish sentient and living things from insentient or non-living; whereas a material object can't do the same as it has no brain or mind. Take an example :– the plants or physical objects are not conscious of themselves and have no mind. Since they have no consciousness, they can't analyse, think, reason, feel good or bad, sense pleasure or pain. It is man with a brain and mind which thinks, reasons, analyses, discriminates, feels good or good, senses pleasure and pain, imagines and worries. An inanimate object doesn't have all these gifts.

You are the real mind or soul, and your body is your possession just as you own an object and that is why you refer to the body with the same way as you refer to any of your objects. The body is really an instrument of the mind through which the mind acts in the world with all sufferings and enjoyments.

Remember that through the respective five sense organs and through the mechanism of the brain that the mind can see, hear, smell, taste and feel. It is anyway the mind which feels the pleasures or pains of the body. It is obvious that if the mind stops or is disconnected from the body instrument, one will feel no pain or pleasure. While sleeping, the mind is dissociated from the body and one never feels pain of one's physical injury. Through the respective physical organs (Karmendriyas), the mind speaks, eats and works.

However, mind and brain are two different things. The brain is a physical organ like any other organ in the body instrument, whereas the mind is a non-physical object. The brain is like a sophisticated and complex computer through which the mind controls and connects itself to the body. Thus the brain acts a connection between the mind and the body. Thus, the brain and body are only instruments of the mind. Remember that the brain and body are made alive and animated only by the access of mind, consciousness and soul. When death comes, the mind or consciousness or soul leaves the physical body and finally the brain and body fall dead and become as any object of this world.

The brain as a physical organ has many parts such as 1. Medulla oblongta. 2. Pituitary gland. 3. Temporary lobe, 4. Optic Chiasm, 5. Pineal glands, 6. Corpus callosum. 7. Cerebrum, 8. Frontal lobe, 9. Cerebral

Cortex. 10. Parrietal Lobe, 11. Occipital lobe and 12 Cerebellum. So the non-physical mind or consciousness or soul resides in it (the brain). As a non-physical thing, mind can't be weighed or quantified in any measurement nor can it be chemically analysed in any lab.

The brain and body, physical in nature, is subject to spoil and perishable and integrated to mother earth, while mind or consciousness or soul remains infinite and never dies. On the contrary, the mind grows with experience and maturity.

As the mind or soul or consciousness are infinite, so they have no beginning and no end. So they are immortal. As they are immortal, they are beyond creation and dissolution, beyond time and space and are eternal. Nothing on earth can touch them.

Mind is indivisible and can't be divided into pieces and acts as a whole. There are people who think that the mind of a child is created out of the mind of parents. This is ridiculous and have no logic because mind or consciousness is not a physical thing and can't be dislodged from parent's consciousness as pieces. Simultaneously some people think that God has divided themselves into separate parts which have become individual souls. This idea has not any logic in it.

The brain needs the source of energy to function; whereas the mind doesn't require any outside energy to work. It is a self deviced energy and self luminous and goes on operating till eternity.

As the mind is much superior to the body, it can act independently of the body. It acts as a master and the body as the servant of the mind. When the body dies, the mind continues to exist as one's basic identity.

To my inspiration and experience, the location of mind or soul is a subtle point of light that locates in the middle of the forehead between the eyebrow called (BHRIKUTTI). In Yoga, this place is called (AJNA CHAKRA). People have a wrong tendency to believe that this place of the soul is in the heart and that all emotions come from the heart. But the place of the soul is in the brain because it is through the brain that it connects to the whole body and the brain functions like a control room of the body. All emotions originate from the mind or soul only. The heart is a physical organ which distributes and clarifies the blood circulation in the body and brain. Finally how can a physical object generate emotions which are non-physical in characteristics?

However, the mind and body are very closely interrelated, so they influence each other. One can feel that any change in the state and health of the body influences the state and health of mind.

Simultaneously, any change in the state or behaviour of the mind has a direct response on the body. We can say clearly that mind and body act and react on each other. But remember that the effect of mind is much more over the body than the effect of the body on the mind.

Now in the Science of Yoga, there is PRANA (vital force or vital energy) in the body. This Prana supplies energy to the physical body for its functioning through a net-work of (NADIS, IDA, PINGALA) spread throughout the body which are also invisible. Prana is also connected to the body on one side and on the other-side to the mind. Any disorder in the balanced and perfect state of the body leads to imbalance in the flow of Prana which in turn affects the balance of mind since Prana is also connected to the mind. Disorder in the balance of state of body can arise due to many types e.g faulty diet, fatigue, laziness and over indulgence in sensual pleasures, wrong style of living, environmental situations, over medication and by using drugs.

Simultaneously, on the other hand, any disorder in the balanced state of mind brings imbalance in the flow of Prana which in turn affects the health of the body since Prana is connected to the body. So disorder in the balanced state of mind can be caused by various negative emotions and vices in mind such as hatred, jealously, anger, greed, revenge, ego, attachment to worldy objects and selfishness etc...

In medical term, the same is described in the term of balance between two components of autonomous nervous system, namely sympathic nervous system. If the balance of the two gets affected, there will be an imbalance created in either the body or in the mind. When one reaches the highest level of spirituality, one can make one's mind wholly immune to bodily afflictions and sufferings. That means one has attained the degree of control over the mind so that one can detach it from the body at will and thus not get affected by it. At this level, ones power of tolerance and mental strength increases to such an extent that one can harmoniously bear a pain which will otherwise break a normal man into pieces.

N.B There are people who develop their mental powers to such an extent that during their life time itself, they can leave their body at their will and travel as far as they want and then come back in their body. So during this travel, they i.e their mind remains in connection to their body by a fine (Silver Cord). This is called Astral travelling. In the event of death, this Silver Cord gets cut off so that the body and mind become totally separated and the body falls dead.

Now there are other mental powers as well such as telepathy, clairvoyance (who can detect distant scenes by mind), (clairaudience who can listen to distant sound of mind) and etc. In these phenomena, the body or the physical senses are not involved. Such phenomena are directly manipulated by the mind only.

In Yoga process, during deep stages of meditation one becomes totally unaware and detached from one's body. That moment if someone talks to the meditator or touches him, he does not notice it because his mind is almost disconnected from the body and the outer world, and has turned towards the Innerself.

## THE STAGES OF THE MIND

The mind is of three stages, which together give the mind a single identity. The three stages of mind are as follows:-

1. Conscious mind, 2. Subconscious mind and 3. Superconscious mind.

1. Conscious Mind:-

The conscious mind is the first stage of the mind which thinks, reasons, discriminates, contemplates and analyses. All sorts of experiences, feelings and emotions such as likes, dislikes, love, hatred, jealousy, anger, joys, sorrows etc are experienced in this part of the mind. Thoughts and imaginations of all types of the future happenings and worrying about the past and future are all concerned through this mind as well.

When studying or practicing RAJA YOGA, one will come to be aware that the conscious mind consists of three faculties; 1. Lower mind. 2. Intellect and 3. Sense of I-ness (that is Ego).

The conscious mind stays in relation with the outside world through the physical five senses, such as sight, sound, smell, touch and taste. And all the voluntarily movements of the body are done by the conscious mind only, through the respective organs of action.

Moreover, the conscious mind stays in touch as well to the subconscious mind. This is the second stage of mind. Notice that the urges and impulses from the subconscious mind influence the conscious mind to act in a certain way and to indulge in certain types of action.

The conscious mind is also exposed to pressure from society and outside world which expects it to act or behave in a certain way in order that its image is not tarnished. There is a conflict if the subconscious mind's impulses, urges and the social expectations don't suit and thus the conscious mind stays in this state of conflict and disturbances, repression then takes place. And if it augments too much, it produces many psychosomatic illnesses.

So the main idea in mind control is to clear these conflicts in these conscious mind by exposing the subconscious mind totally and removing all sorts of biases, prejudices, fears, suspicions and negative emotions and feelings, such like greed, anger, jealousy, envy's. Wrong desires, lust, revenge and hatred, which are all accumulated there.

2. Subconscious Mind:-

This subconscious mind is another stage of mind and one gets aware of it when one goes deep inside the Inner journey. This process also is done through Yoga Sadhana.

The storehouse of the memory is inside of the subconscious mind. All things that one has seen, heard, thought, talked, done either in this life or in earlier lives get stored in the subconscious mind as a sort of permanent record. The emotions which are linked to thoughts, speech and deeds or actions are also being stored in the subconscious mind altogether with the memory. However it is the same emotions which record the thoughts, words and deeds, which after having been accumulated in this subconscious mind that really reveal chaos or confusion within people's live. (This is called the reaction of past KARMA). So the conscious mind becomes restless by regularly being disturbed from below due to these past emotions. They are like a whirlpool which is kept under the conscious mind. The impulses are urges emerging from the subconscious mind, regularly requesting satisfaction through the conscious mind. It is the emotions that turn the vibration of the subconscious mind are impure, then turmoil provokes the conscious mind. The past incidental reactions which react with emotions create urges on the subconscious mind and these are called impressions. And due to these impressions that people have different sorts of tendencies, inclinations, habits, biases, phobias, fears etc. In the Science of Yoga, the mind controls all these impressions and impurities which are being purified from the subconscious mind.

Never generalize any past events good or bad in your mind. As one man may be good to you, but bad to others and vice versa. He needs to purify the subconscious mind from all biases and prejudices of the past conditioning and should not let emotion play havoc with the conscious mind. This is no direct route to the subconscious mind and the only way to go to it is by the conscious mind. But the only way to have direct access to it is by self-hypnotism, by making the conscious mind in a semi-sleepy or drowsy state by suitable science techniques, either one believes it or not. Mental powers and occult powers all belong to the subconscious mind. Telepathy, clairvoyance, clairaudience, hypnosis, visualisation and auto-suggestion all these phenomena belong to the subconscious mind. Here also by any way of meditation, one can have access to the subconscious mind and can have access to these powers as well. Finally the power of materializing of thoughts also belongs to the field of the subconscious mind. And this is to bear in mind that the autonomous nervous system in the body is completely under the control of the subconscious mind, such as the activities of breathing, digestion, blood circulation, heart, immune system etc.

3. The Superconscious Mind:-

Superconscious mind is the reality of a peaceful and blissful mind without impurities and it is the real Self. Even for a moment in the super-conscious mind, one can explain the peaceful moment. The more one stays in the fountain of joy and peace, the more the nectar of bliss and peace one will have. The real self is the real everlasting peace and happiness. The delusive pleasures and happiness which come from material possessions and sensory enjoyments are only momentary and full of pain.

How to be in contact with the superconscious mind or the real Self? Here the superconscious mind performs as a veil between the conscious mind and the superconscious mind and prevents the conscious mind from seeing or feeling the superconscious mind directly by penetrating inside.

An example is being set to illustrate this. The subconscious mind is like a river filled with water; the superconscious mind is the bottom of the river and the conscious mind is the perceiver looking from the surface through the water of the river.

So as long as the water of the river is turbulent and dirty (i.e the subconscious mind is full of impurities), the conscious mind can't see the bottom of the river. But when the water is pure and tranquil i.e a pure subconscious mind purified of all impurities, one can clearly see the bottom of the river.

So here it is clear that the techniques of Self-Realization are nothing but a discipline of cleaning the impurities of the subconscious mind and a practice to still the conscious mind to turn it inward. In common and ordinary man, the conscious mind is most of the time focussed outwards and it is in contact with the world. So here when it is inwardly guided, it is directed towards the real self (Superconscious mind). Meditation helps one to go inward oneself, that is towards the Real Self.

## THE CONDITIONS OF CONSCIOUSNESS:-

The waking condition of consciousness: This is to inform that there are different conditions of consciousness in which one's mind or consciousness can manifest itself. When one is wide awake to this material world around oneself, thinking, analyzing, reasoning, feeling about things, one is said to be in a state of waking of consciousness. That is the state in which one's conscious mind is fully activated and remained alert.

However, there is the ASC (Altered condition of consciousness). There are other conditions of consciousness in which one's conscious mind goes to sleep or semi-sleep, drowsy state and one's subconscious or unconscious mind takes over. Furthermore, there are some conditions in which one's subconscious mind also becomes motionless.

Some of these altered conditions of consciousness are being mentioned and elaborated now:-

1.  The dream condition:- here the conscious mind goes to sleep, but remember that the subconscious mind stays activated.

2.  Profound sleep condition:– here both the subconscious and the conscious mind are at complete relaxation.

3.  The Hypnotic state:- now in this condition, the conscious mind is hushed into a semi sleep or drowsiness by a hypnotist man through his particular techniques and then he takes control over the subconscious mind of his subject and gets many useful past information from it and then, rectifies the behaviour of his

subject by implementing new suggestions in the subconscious mind.

4. Self Hypnosis:- in self-hypnosis, one becomes the operator of one's subconscious mind. Here one stills one's conscious mind by performing many techniques to have an access to one's subconscious mind and then one gives useful suggestion to one's subconscious mind to correct many behavioural deficiencies in oneself. And in this condition, one fully remains aware of oneself unlike the other states of consciousness as already mentioned above when one loses one's consciousness in this self-hypnosis process.

5. Here the Yogic way of meditation:– While meditates, one first has to still the conscious mind and then the subconscious mind, and afterwards reaches the superconsciousness condition with full awareness. Please bear in mind that in deep sleep, both conscious mind and subconscious mind are calm, but since one has no awareness, one steps into an unconscious condition rather than to the condition of superconsciouness.

Here to be noted that by using many drugs one can also alter the condition of the consciousness. These drugs respond as the RAS (Reticular Activating System) in part of the brain which is concerned with the waking, sleep conditions and accordingly brings the unconscious mind to a sort of drowsiness. But remember that these drugs have many side-effects and definitely they weaken the mind condition.

Anyway if one proceeds in the situation of mental control, one should usually attempt those conditions of consciousness where one stays aware of oneself or on the other hand one stays under full control of oneself. However, this aids in powering the mind. But in these conditions where one becomes passive and leaves oneself to the control of others, one is not strengthening one's mind. Rather one is weakening it and making it subject to others' influences.

Remember that through the practice of concentration and meditation, one can overcome the obstructions to the path of Yoga. Concentration leads to meditation and when one goes in deep meditation, this is called SAMADHI or the superconscious condition. And breathings as well are helpful in quieting the modification of the minds and the central nervous system. When the mind becomes absolutely still, the spirit reigns supreme in its own glory. That state is very difficult to attain because the mind is vacillating too much, sometimes it is happy and sometimes unhappy etc, and performing all sorts of actions.

The mind has manifold desires. It rushes the body towards the fulfilment of desires, acquiring certain experiences which go down in the mind and remain there in the subconscious mind in seed form. Then it goes to sleep. It wakes up again and performs the same thing. In this way, it is dancing around from one incarnation to another. There is no stop for a moment. If one tries to stop it, one shall find it very difficult. One's will-power is not so strong enough to control it. But in cases where the will-power has been developed to such an extent that it can command the mind to stop, then the mind obeys the command. And those persons who achieve this state are called Yogis.

Here what I want to clarify is that concentration, meditation and superconsciousness are the three important steps and principal states of Yoga. Concentration leads to meditation, and meditation leads to the superconsciousness state in one's daily life. If someone applies these states, he is the only one to be near and divine himself. He can be a Christ, Krishna or Prophet or Sage or Yogi. It is not easy I know, but not impossible, as practice makes perfect. One can concentrate upon something that one can perceive with one's senses, or that has a form. So one can easily concentrate upon some business proposition or some mathematical problem. But when it comes to try to concentrate on one's mind, upon something which is unknown, it becomes very difficult. For instance, when one says God is the spirit, or the spirit is residing within one, one does not know what the spirit is like. One cannot form a mental concept of the spirit, and for that purpose, it is very difficult to think about it. But the only way is to know, first of all, what one's Ego or Self is.

Remember that the nature of real spirit is beyond one's thoughts, beyond time, space, and causation and therefore it is very difficult to make a mental concept of the spirit. One cannot think about it. One can try to think, but the mind fails, because the mind is ordinarily accustomed to think within certain limitations of form or within time and space.

Now one cannot think of anything without repeating its name. If one tries to think of a friend, one cannot hold the thoughts of a friend, without repeating the name of the friend. When one is thinking of a friend, one is mentally repeating friend, friend, friend or otherwise one's mind will be distracted by different things. One holds one's attention and interest by repetition of the name. You will notice that in all religions the repetition of the name of the Lord is considered to be a great help in concentrating, namely by counting the beads and the repeating of prayers. All these in a way are helpful in the life of common people.

After all, we are all moving towards the big knowledge, wisdom and realization of the Divinity in this life or in the next life to come. Here realization does not come by reading books. One may read scriptures through one's life and study the nature of creation or become an intellectual or scientist, but that will no not do any good. One has to understand the meaning. Take one word of the scripture, analyse it and go down into the state of sueprconsciousness. Try to feel it. The word God, for instance, or infinite spirit or absolute spirit, or love for divine wisdom, anything like that and concentrate one's mind upon it. Think about it, meditate on it and when one enters into the superconscious state; one becomes conscious of the meaning. Then one begins to feel it. The moment we begin to feel it, one is in the state of superconsciousness. That is really called realization. And through this realization, one can become as Sage or Prophet himself in the new future. We all have these precious pearl within us, but we must go deep and find it within ourself.

After all, it is not the sins that are holding anyone down; sins are the errors or hideous things that appear in darkness because one does not know the law. These are the works of the mind that is ignorant; and that ignorance is the original sin. So this ego is born in ignorance and one may metaphorically say that it was born in original sin and it must be crucified, and that to-day is the day to crucify it at this altar of God. Crucify one's ignorant and sinful ego. After having crucified the sin and ego, the resurrection will come into one.

Remember that the aim of Raja Yoga is to help one to rise above this ordinary sense consciousness of the ordinary mortal ego and transcend all the realms of thought and nature into the superconscious state.

Now before I move into the control of mind and its techniques, I would like to give you a brief concept of the SOUL itself and the conditions of the mind and its brain waves through EEG (electro encephalograms) apparatus.

33

SOUL:-

The soul is all the constituents of the levels of mind put together. So it is clear that the soul and mind consciousness are not different things: Existence of soul apart from mind or consciousness has no significance since consciousness is the essential sign of soul which is expressed through operations of mind. Remember the saying:- "*I think therefore I am*" *of Descartes* If one can't think, feel and has no awareness about oneself, that is one doesn't have a mind, so what is the significance of the existence of a separate soul? So here one can imagine that soul is the real I or the essential identity. Whereas body is only a possession of soul and not its true identity. And it is clear that body, brain, head and organs are only the instruments. And that's why one uses the terms of one's body, head and brain. If there is no mind, therefore no soul exists and vice versa.

In order to come to know the soul, one must attain to the highest point of superconsciousness, then it will be able to understand this matter of soul, mind superconsciousness or realization. After all, it is through the mind levels that one has to practice Yoga to reach the soul or supersoul as one may put it.

Our scientists have proved that the brain discharges electrical waves or vibrations of different frequencies in different conditions of mind. This is measured by an apparatus which is called EEG (electro encephallograms) and the heart is being measured by the ECG (electrocardiograms).

1. When one is widely awake and busy in worldly activities, the brain waves are of the frequency of 14 to 21 Hz and are called beta waves.

2. When one is quite in relaxed condition, the frequency of brain waves is between the rank of 8 to 13 Hz and called alpha waves.

3. When one is in a dream, the brain frequency is between the rank of 4 to 7 Hz and or called theta waves.

4. When one is in deep sleep, the brain waves frequency is between 0-3 Hz and are called delta waves.

Finally when one is in deep meditation the frequency of the waves goes in diminishing as stated above and although they remain completely conscious during meditation, one can still reach to delta state i.e 0-3 Hz. During ordinary meditation the mind remains as mentioned in the second phase that is alpha waves 8 to 13 Hz. So here it is clear that the deeper one meditates by improving the quality of meditation, the better one can also improve health of mind and can gain a complete control of mind.

**Control of the mind and its methods:-**

Control of the mind is definitely the most difficult thing in the world but the most rewarding thing as well, if one can master it. Therefore, it is possible by continuous perseverance, practice and adoption of the proper Yoga techniques. It is also said that one can stop the wind from blowing, even the river can be topped from flowing, but one can't control one's mind.

One can learn and practise it from some one who has perfectly controlled his own mind. That's why a Guru is the most important person in this situation. One must have a great deal of skill, alertness, sense of humour, goodness of heart, sense of strategy, patience and regular practice at the same hours daily and some heroic flair which makes it possible and not get discouraged or disheartened in the face of thousand drawbacks.

In the famous spiritual book of Krishna, the **Geeta:-** he mentions that the only two ways to control the mind is to adopt the two disciplines and secrets of Arjuna:-

1.  ABHYASA (The Yoga of practice).

2.  VAIRAGYA:- The Yoga of disinterestedness. And by using these above practices sincerely, the mind can be tamed, and become one's slave. Keep on and up the practice and one will find that one's mind will follow in whatever direction one leads it. Remember that the mind is like a white material just returned from the laundry. It will be red if dipped in red dye and yellow if dipped in yellow colour; it will definitely have whatever colour one dips it in.

The fundamental point which everyone needs to remember is that the only bondage is the mind and freedom is also of the mind as well. If one has control over one's mind, one becomes one's own king and master of this world and universe.

**Practice and dispassion are the whole secret of mind control:-**

There are three practices to follow to conquer the monkey mind.

1.  One must understand and study the nature of the mind.

2.  One must develop a strong will-power to control the mind.

3.  One must learn certain Yoga techniques and practise them earnestly and intelligently.

In brief, we all have this will within ourselves, but sometimes this will to control the mind is not very strong. So the will to control the mind can never be strong until and unless one has deliberately and irrevocably renounced worldly pleasures as one of the main pursuits of life. **This infection that eats away the vitality of the will to control the mind is the pursuit of seeking pleasure and enjoying pleasure. It is only by going beyond pleasure and pain that one can attain joy and bliss.** One has to practise renunciation which means by giving up the enjoyment of sense pleasure and the contentment arising from the "*unripe ego.*"

Finally the most important thing is to strengthen the will-power to such a highest point that even in the face of repeated failures, one is not disheartened or disappointed, rather than with every new failure to control the mind, one is aroused to fresh attempt with new and fresh enthusiasm and fervour.

Remember the saying of Buddha:-

"If one man conquers in battle a thousand men a thousand times, and if another conquers himself, he the latter is the greatest conqueror."

Occasional or repeated failures to control the mind must not be taken too seriously.

**How does the attraction of sense pleasures die away?**

When one realizes the consummation of all happiness and all pleasures in God who is the indivisible eternal ocean bliss. Those who enjoy Him can find no attraction in the cheap worthless pleasures of the world.

Before proceeding further with the methods of controlling the mind, I have an advice which is of precious importance to anyone. Some of the teachers or persons directly teach the pupil with advanced meditation techniques for controlling the mind, but people having highly scattered and restless minds find this direct methods of meditation more difficult and become discouraged or disheartened because it is clear that they are not capable to still their mind even for a fraction. And in the end, they feel more restless during this meditation techniques and want to get up as soon as possible from meditation and feel very dejected and can experience a negative result and lose hope for that way of teaching is not what it should be due to ignorance.

It is advisable to such people of wavering and weak mind to start controlling the mind by practicing physical methods which don't require total stoppage of thought processes and need only mild concentration relaxation, posture (Asana) Pranayama (breathing exercises) and then gradually they can move to more rigorous methods of mind control.

**Physical techniques**

First of all, the physical methods are developed in a simple way, for the mind and body complex are closely interrelated and once one is able to practise them, the body can be controlled as well as the mind. The twelve organs, the muscles, nerves, tendous artery, tendons and veins should be really in good condition and relaxed by doing simple postures and breathing exercises.

## 1. ASANAS – Postures and Exercises:-

One should perform or practise postures and various stretching exercises. When stretching and relaxing all various muscles, tensions and stress deposited in them are relieved, leading to the free flow of PRANA (Vital Energy) which leads to calmness and mind control. Here remember that if the muscles are tense and contracted and hard, Prana (vital energy) is not able to pass freely and this has corresponding effect on the balance of the body and mind complex, because mind and Prana are closely interlinked.

Finally aerobic exercises involving quiet movements, release of tension accumulated in the body here and there and this also leads to a better flow of Prana and better functioning of the mind. If the mind and body complex are free from all tensions and impurities, that means one is healthy and one's life is with joy and is beyond pleasure and pain.

## 2. PRANAYAMA (Breathing Exercises).

The breath has a great effect on the mind and body. They both are interlinked. So here when the mind is disturbed, breath also becomes irregular, unrhythmic, noisy, jerky, shallow and limited to upper chest only. But when the mind is calm and relaxed, the breath is deep, slow, rhythmic and the abdominal involving movement of diaphram. This process of mind and breath is also done vice versa, i.e by changing the breathing so as to match it with a relaxed condition of mind, one can calm one's mind.

When one is practicing various breathing exercises, the Prana Shakti is greatly increased which leads to a great control and strengthening of the mind. It is to be noted here that Nadi Shodhana is a breathing exercise that is specially effective for the balance of mind and central Nervous System.

N.B:- A list of breathing exercises and postures will be added in the end of this book and one can refer to any good book of the same.

## 3. SOME KRIYAS (PURIFICATION TECHNIQUES)

Kriyas form part of Yoga and they are called neti such as jalneti, sutra neti, kunjal etc.. And there are the eyes exercises also TRATAKA is done with concentration either with a candle or flower or picture.

This is very useful for the eyes and concentration. The Kriyas have been specially aroused to clean the body impurities. When there are no impurities in the body, the Prana flows freely and mind becomes calm and quiet.

## 4. RELAXING AND SITTING POSTURES:-

Padmasana, Siddhasana, Swastikasana, Sukhasana are few postures to calm the mind for meditation. If these postures are mastered, one can sit effortlessly in them for any duration of time. Remember that in these asanas (postures) the spine becomes straight and correctly aligned.

When one sits in these above mentioned postures without moving for a period of time, one can feel that the mind becomes centred and controlled and stays quiet. While the body is motionless, so the mind also becomes quiet because of its interlinked with the body.

When one is in the straight vertical spine, it encourages Prana (vital force) to rise upwards against its normal tendency of flowing downwards during other activities. With practice one achieves a higher level of consciousness and its strength and control are greatly improved.

## 5. FOOD OR DIET

To bear in mind food has also a great role to play on the mind. Here the food is of 3 types and forms part of Yoga.

### 1. Satwic Food:-

By consuming satvic food, it is said that Prana (vital force) runs clearly and properly in the body and mind is kept, calm, positive and under control. These satvic foods are:- fruits, vegetable, milk, honey, brown sugar, brown rice, whole grains, pulses, cereal, yogurt, dry fruit or nuts etc..

## 2. Rajasic Foods:-

Stimulate the mind to become restless and remain always occupied, if not one feels bored with nothing to do. And one becomes tense. These foods are tea, coffee, tobacco, cigarette, cola drinks, sugar, salt, onion, garlic, fresh fish, eggs and meat as well.

## 3. Tamasic Foods:-

They are meats, stale food, onion, alcohol, fatty and fried foods etc… These foods make the mind dull and lethargic, very restless and tense. An example is to see the way the lion acts in the forest.

One must know what type of food to consume and when one must eat, how much one eats, and what combination of food one must eat and at what temperature. Remember that too hot or too cold food is not good for the digestion system.

## Getting away with the wrong foods out of the kitchen:-

The first thing which one has to do, is to throw out the wrong foods that have been the problems in the past and which would get in one's way in the future. One should throw them out or give them away, but the importance is to get them completely out of the daily uses and out of the kitchen.

However, I know it is very hard for a hungry man to chalk any food products away, no matter how unhealthy it may be. Go on a real search and cut the habits of consuming the high fat food. They are as follows:-

1. Any meat, poultry or fish products.

2. All dairy products, including butter, milk or cream, yogurt and cheese.

3. Margarine

4. Even vegetable oil or olive oil should be consumed at a moderate and minimum way.

5. All salad dressings other than non-fat dressing.

6. Cookies, cakes, pies and ice cream, other than non-fat.

7. Potato chips and lot of fried foods.

8. Minimum nuts and nuts butter.

9. Sugary candies.

In the end one will feel a certain sense of relief as one gets rid of these unhealthy products within few months of not using them (Wrong food as mentioned above).

Now I am including as to my knowledge 20 food items which one can consume without any fear and one can consume them in virtually unlimited servings.

With these 20 foods one can feel free to eat in very generous portions and as much as one wants. In fact, there are many more than the above number. But remember to eat them without butter, margarine, or oily toping of fats.

They are as follows:-

Corn, Rice, Potatoes, lettuce, Broccoli, Carrots, Black beans, Kidney beans, spinach, lentils and pulses, celery, peas, cauliflower, pineapple, cabbage, oranges, apples, grapefruits, Bananas, oatmeal and wheats.

This is my advice as a clue, it is up to you to seek and accept your own diets in the daily life.

## 6. FASTING :-

It is also quite clean that fasting as well plays an important role in the mind. First the impurities of the body are being taken away and this leads to a balanced flow of Prana (vital energy). Secondly, one has to exercise one's will power not to give in to the temptation of food. And this helps in the development of mind control and the strengthening.

## 7. ENVIRONMENTAL CONDITIONS :-

It is of great help to make sure that your surroundings are favourable to the good mental health. We should consider the climatic conditions, temperature, humidity, ventilation, sun light, noise levels, colors and the cleanliness of the surroundings-all these can affect mental health. Finally, it is clear that negative surrounding-situations can also sometimes counter-balance the effort in the mind control

## 8. SILENCE:-

This also is very important as it plays a role in the increasing of mental power. Nowadays, many people play the fools and a lot of energy is being evaporated during gossips, arguments, discussions and unnecessary talks of non-sense about others; people poke their nose in what is none of their business. But silence conserves a lot of mind energy. It is very difficult to remain silent but practically it is possible to stay silent all the time. But one must at least remain in complete silence some time during the day. And following this, one can also read, write, listen to smooth music during the day as well.

## 9. CELIBACY:-

This is as well an important topic in helping to control the mind. Remember that many people are biased with the celibacy factor. Here celibacy is not meant that one has to abstain completely from sex and as most people misinterprit. However, sex is a natural thing and process in nature, and a natural biological urge and its strong suppression might create many sorts of complications such as physiological and psychological diseases. In celibacy, one should not become a slave to this or any urge. One should enjoy it like a master and prevent it from controlling one. One must constantly think that one is bigger than sex and that it is in one's hand to get sensual pleasure and for procreation, and that it can't be that important and bigger that one itself. Enjoy it but don't get attached and identified with it and should keep one superior standing when compared to sex.

There is a spiritual saying which goes like that:- Enjoy the world, but don't let the world over-throw you. Or one may eat food but don't let the food eat one. This vital energy (Prana) which is spent through sex makes the mind weak. So by preserving this energy through regular control of sex helps in the upliftment of the human brain, and mind and body complex.

Before ending, the mind control and methods, I want to introduce to you two items of Yoga which are of utmost importance in one's daily life if practice is done regularly and with perseverance, one can reach the highest level in spirituality.

They are as following :

## 1. Trataka:–

The concentration posture in Yoga Kriya. It is a very effective Yoga item and it strengthens and centers the mind of the practitioner. How it is done and practised? It is done by fixing at a certain object or picture, deity or light, etc continuously with the open eyes at a distance of 2 and 3 feet, till tears start to come down the eyes. One should sit with folded legs or on the chair with spine, neck, and head straight. It is proved that it is a very good Yoga posture for strengthening and removing impurities of the eyes. But it should be practised by people who have good eyes.

1. The Yoga posture is the Omkar or Pranava:– This is the mysterious monosyllable. `Om' is the womb for everything. All the sacred scriptures of the Hindus, are contained in `Om' as is used by Hindus, as Amen is used by Christian at the end of prayers, Muslims use the word Ahmeen during prayers. Amen or Ahmeen are all modifications of Om. In Hindus, the Hum is the modification of Om as well. Om is Guru's voice as well. Om is the soul of souls and the light of lights.

However, the sound Om and Hum have been found very effective in the controlling and calming the disturbed and distracted mind due to the powerful effects of vibration produced by these sounds. The methods to practice them is that one should inhale deeply and then exhale slowly through the mouth making the sound O, make this sound as loud and as lengthy as possible. At the end close one's lips pronouncing M or humming sound that is the first one and the second the humming only is done in this way, both the nostrils and exhale slowly through the nose only making the sound of humming like bees from the throat while keeping the lips closed. That is the bees sound demonstration.

Remember that Yoga postures are all derived from the natural law, that is Nature itself is a great Guru.

**Mental techniques and processes.**

In mental techniques, the will-power is used to alter some aspects of the personality. These physical techniques of mind control finally make it even easy to exercise such will-power.

## 1. Concentration:-

It is a certitude that concentration increases the mind strength. When the mind becomes strong, there is nothing to affect or disturb it, no matter the trials and odds life. Nothing such as sorrow or joy can touch a strong mind. But if it is a weak mind, that becomes the slavery of all ups and downs in daily life. Remember to improve concentration, and whatever works, duty or activities that one is involved in, one should try to be wholly absorbed in them, however simple or ordinary it may be. Once one is deeply involved in them, even the whole world at this time is dead for him. It is also an example that while reading a book or any other task, one should be totally involved in it. Also one should study to concentrate on any interesting thing to develop true control of mind. Concentration aims at a positive single-mindedness, which is a desirable feature for success and happiness in one's daily life. Most of the time, however, people are preoccupied with either past problems and memories or in the future anticipations and never think of the present, eventually their power of concentration is blurred and the mind becomes weak.

## 2. Forgetfulness, Detachment and Discrimination:-

While one is concentrating, one at the same time should create the ability to detach oneself from anything or any task at a moment notice. Many people can concentrate and involve in a task, but they find it hard to forget this first activity completely while taking on to the coming one. It seems as a hangover moment and this only shows that one gets unduly attached to many things which one should not do. This world is like a stage with worldly things and interests for us to get necessary training and lessons from them for one's growth. One uses them for one's learning and growth, but should not get attached to them. Once the purpose is attained by the necessary lessons, one should forget and discard them. Remember well that both concentration and detachment should be practised together.

**Swami Vivekananda has said:-**

"The ability to forget and detach from undesirable past is a great quality for achieving success in life. Though it is sometimes useful to remember but it is often wise to forget."

In point of fact, nothing is really forgotten, as all things of the past get stored in the subconscious mind.

Finally one has to really practise discrimination, that is one should at any moment differentiate between from what is good and what is wrong. This is hard but one should do this to purify the mind from bad thoughts, the mind is a devil workshop, remember well. One should dominate the mind with constant positive thinking and not get dominated by negative and bad thinking which weakens the mind.

### 3. The thinking must be planned.

This must be assured at any moment and intervals, the thinking must be systematically organized or planned, but not haphazardly and at random or unsystematically. Haphazard thinking which is unplanned and people of day dreaming are examples of fickle and fragmented mind. And when the mind is fickle, fragmented and weak, this shows that instead of controlling the subconscious mind, one is being controlled by it. So here the conscious mind must be in complete activeness with complete awareness. That is the conscious mind must retain itself in a status of masterly and control its servant, the subconscious mind. One must be aware that by keeping the mind into passive, idle, and day-dreaming habits, the influence of the subconscious mind dominates the conscious mind. However, one should make sure that the thoughts in the mind are truly needed at the present moment. It has been proved that most people waste their life in futile thinking. Finally any present moment can be easily used to think positively for good activities in one's daily life.

### 4. Master over the urges and impulses. Be patient and self-control and self-restraint.

Make sure that one is not driven away by urges and impulses in the daily life. When one is swayed by the urges and impulses of daily life, that means one has a weak mind. Realize that one must daily check and control the mind and don't get entangled and become its slave. Be a great master of one's mind. It is good to know that whatever the urges and impulses entering the mind, it is clear that all these come from one's conscious mind. Often we are unaware of all the desires, passions and tendencies dormant in us. Don't take it for granted. One has to examine it clearly first and then hold it for some time or ignore it completely. And finally by practising patience and perseverance regularly in this way, one's will power and energy and strength will expand.

Here whenever one wants to increase one's will power, one should try to use such a method of patience everywhere and at any moment, and try to avoid anxiety, desperation and hurry in worldly matters and sensual pleasures. Be sure that one can practise tolerance and patience no matter people's remarks, insults or criticism about one instead of reacting frantically without proper examination. Finally this also adds to the strength of one's mind. And nowadays the world is going so fast that everybody is getting lost in this material and illusive sphere and finally they forget themselves, who they really are. Running after the material, their mind is weakened and all sorts of diseases, mentally and physically, are being created. Lots and lots of hospitals and private clinics are being opened in order to combat human diseases, yet these health problems get festered. It seems that the subject of health is being infinite and it goes on and on without an end.

Mental attitudes should be altered and positive thinking must be adopted. The most important phase in one's life is, how one thinks. It is one's way of thinking which builds up one's character and individuality or personality in daily life. One must foster the habit of scanning everything in a positive way, even the most harassing or miserable conditions. The mind gets weakened by thinking negatively, when then it becomes restless, agitated and impure. One should alter every single negative situation into positive thinking by adjusting again the mind attitude gradually. There is a very positive way of doing it, that is suppose one abuses you or throws some unpleasant remarks in anger, so instead of reacting negatively about him, just think that his attitude is upset at this moment or he is still not fully mature, that's why he is behaving like this. In this case, don't create any spiteful action or thinking against him. This is what is called a positive and good thinking or attitude.

If one cultivates a positive thinking, one will definitely attract favourable physical situations and create a good environment. According to the law of psychic attraction, one attracts physical conditions and circumstances towards one according to one's thoughts. For example, if one repeats regularly the thinking of not catching any special illness, one will find that the symptoms of that disease start appearing and one can find that such is the force of thoughts in oneself. One can find the truth in this above fact.

So by regularly thinking positively, one creates an atmosphere or an aura or a vibration of positive conditions around, which benefit not only one, but all others around coming in one's contact. And if you are strongly positive practically and theoretically, these good vibrations protect you from the contamination of any negative act or thinking discharged by others.

**Now to end with, I am giving you a brief idea of the spiritual ways to get the mind calmed and controlled.**

The four paths of Yoga are as follows:-

1. Raja Yoga – Meditation.

2. Karma Yoga – Action without fruit or disinterested actions.

3. Bhakti Yoga – Japam and constant thinking of God name.

4. Gyana Yoga – Realization of self-knowledge and the supreme (God) in the world.

1. **Raja Yoga:**– To know oneself by meditation. This is a key to the control of mind. In meditation one turns down all the thoughts of mind from the material world and guides them towards the internal, that is inwards. This form of meditation is practised by a special way of concentration in which one fixes one's mind on a single point that is the Ajna chakra (the middle of the frontal head between eyebrows, or any picture or deity etc, etc.. This is a method done with sitting postures and straightened spine column, in a straight position and this helps to quieten the mind and make it to turn inwards. When this state of mind is being regularly practised, the subconscious desires, impurities, and emotions get functioned and operated and started to rise to the surface of consciousness. So at this moment one witnesses them as a spectator and they are released from one's consciousness. Then slowly the subconscious mind is purified from all impurities, desires, phobia, emotions, passions, fears etc and turned pure and clear as a crystal. In this condition, one can clearly see one's real self, the superconscious mind and imbibes from it as much nectar of peace, power of divinity and bliss as possible. And it is clear that one becomes a Self-Realized man with a determined mastery over one's mind. Nothing on earth, I mean nothing of external situation or circumstance, can then affect the balance of the mind. And finally one climbs much above the petty worldly material things and one becomes as a lotus flower blossoming blissfully in the dirts of this material world.

2. **Karma Yoga:**- Action without fruit, disinterestedness, Unselfishness. This Karma (Karmic law) action also relieves man from the purity of mind. It is done with selfless actions in one's duty in daily life. One accepts each and all works as an order from the divine and the action is being performed sincerely and as the offering as a servant of God and respects to God as the real doer and without

any personal benefit. One does it as a service to God and to the world as well. By adopting this habit and positive attitude, one is guided to a general purification of the mind.

**3. Bhakti Yoga** - Thinking of God with all day breath, that is continuous remembrance of God. By remembrance of God regularly, a kind of mysterious relation is built up between one and God by the righteousness of which the fragrance of peace, purity, bliss, knowledge and strength begin to accelerate in one from God and this simultaneously purifies and strengthens one's mind. The more one approaches God consciously, the more rapidly does one's mind get purified due to the flow of divine attributes. The practice of continuously remember the Almighty is to try to feel His presence while eating, talking, working, sleeping, travelling as if one is eating with Him, travelling, talking with Him and sleeping with Him.

In whatever one does or thinks, one feels as if God is in front of one. Let one feel that one is involved with Him in all one's activities. Remember to make Him one of the partners in all one does and never feels lonely. Believe everything in terms of the Almighty. That is the way of how a discipline is in the practice of Bhakti Yoga; it clears one's mind and finally reaches perfection, that is God realization. Be very careful the moment one is in complete and sincere remembrance of God; one becomes very strong and powerful man and have direct relation to God and one should be cautious in bestowing any abuse or harm to one. It is not that I am getting you to be frightened, but it is the truth. As you know quite well, "what one sows, one reaps the same from it." What I mean is to be very cautious as these bhaktas do not harm any one in whatever situation. Such people are very calm and harmless in whatever situation. Beware that you do not harm or abuse anyone, else one will have to pay for the consequences in this life itself.

**4. Gyana Yoga**:- Realization of the Self.

This way of enlightenment is normally applicable and suits the intellectuals. One has to deal with study of contemplation, discussion and enquiry to know and understand the real and true nature of oneself, God and the mysteries of material world. Finally if one comes to discover the truth and mysteries of life, all the doubts, fears, complexes, worries, anxieties, phobias completely disintegrate, and this leads one to the whole purification of the mind. Such a man is not an ordinary one, not a slave to this material world. He is the king of kings. He is his own master and nothing affects him in this sludge and fake world during this life.

**This is to conclude that there are two types of character in man:-**

1.  The first one has achieved awareness and attained the highest, self realization. His mind is pure and calm and he is full of love and serves others with love without any distinctions. His actions are without any expectation. There are very few people of this group in the material world.

2.  The second one is those people who are ignorant and always look miserable and unsatisfied, even with wealth and strong body at their possession; they often and always find faults with others. Their minds are always weak with ego and selfishness and become a slave to senses and while doing actions, they always want to get something in return. The overwhelming majority are found in this second category.

Remember that we are all the instruments in God's hand. But one who has realized that he is an instrument in the hand of God becomes a real instrument in His hand without even feeling the need of having to say or think so.

One must be inspired by Truth, and Truth must become one's guiding life itself just as the breath that is inspired becomes one's life. And then as an instrument one must live the Truth and one becomes the living Truth and finally one's life is transformed into the divine. Truth has to be actualized; it has to be lived at any second of one's life. It should be practised both in theory and practice. Unfortunately the intellect does not comprehend the totality as one, but divides it.

In Gita, Krishna has said:-

*"Man attains perfection by regarding every one of his actions as a flower offered at the omnipresent feet of God."*

*"This body is your temple not my body and all the enjoyments that it goes through everyday are your worship. Sleep itself is Samadhi.. You are the one that is the reality in this temple. When the legs walk they world around your temple and whatever the mouth utters is all your praise. Thus, O Lord whatever I do is thus God adoration."* To follow this, one must have the practice of idol-worship in order to have this inner-feeling.

However, Yoga practices are only aids, not the master key. In my experience, the master key is to adapt, adjust, accommodate, accept and regular practise sadhana. Nowadays, only rituals and ceremonies are being used as prayers in temples, mosques, churches, pagoda etc. As God is everywhere and within everything, He is not only installed in all the above places. People should instead follow and practise the teachings of all these Sages, Prophets and Swamis, Yogis and Avatars. But it is a pity to see that people have completely and totally ignored their teachings but built organizations and temples for them, and make of prayers a ritual only these are only in theory without sincere practice which should be carried on inwardly and not by mere show of going to pray.

Finally one is misled and forgets oneself and gets immersed in this material and fake world, one becomes the slave of it till death do part them off.

One may still stay in this world and make it a paradise, by detaching and discriminating the monkey mind with actions carried out without expecting any results in returning. One should diminish the Ego and be like a lotus flower as an example.

When the mind is free, detached, discriminating and calm , nothing on earth can prevent it from reaching the highest goal in life. We all have come from Him, we must make our duty to return to Him, the

Almighty. We must break that circle of birth and death. It is in this human form that we can do it, while not any species of this universe have this precious gem to get out of this circle of birth and death. We are fortunate to be born in this human form. It is really a precious chance.

Here to end, it is not our aspiration, endeavour and hope to worship a Saint. We are only trying to inhale the nectar of the perfume of these Saints or enlightened men or gurus, inorder to have the perfume from them. It might work in our own souls, it might bring about within us an enfoldment to the extent we deserve and in the manner in which it is to happen to us. It should be just like food eaten which nourishes the living body, even so it is possible that these truths absorbed through our ears and eyes, organs and nooks and corners of the body may also be assimilated into our very goals and finally may become the living truth in us, the Truth that lives. So we all have the great chance to imbibe their teachings and types of spiritual living to reach this goal and rare gem. This is possible by doing spiritual theory and practices in our daily life. All is within us, believe me.

As I have said and emphasized, it is by practice that one becomes perfect. So here theory and practice must go hand in hand; one is not the enemy hand in hand. One is not the enemy of the other, but the friend and one without the other is useless.

Now Sankirtan, Bhajan or Japam alone are not enough. If really analysed, all these lead to emotionalism but there must be some Jnana, some understanding. Kirtan is singing God's name with pure heart and mind, not conducting a musical competition. It is the Bhavana that is most important and one must learn to recognise and understand that Bhavana. The practice is extremely important, but not without understanding.

To end here may Thy God bless thee and be with you all the way round in your daily life. One should practise Yoga for the purpose of self-purification.

One might have a frail body and be unhealthy but if one's mind is pure, calm and strong with a complete awareness, one can realize the inner-self and reach the highest perfection in this only human life.

Secondly, one might have a strong and healthy body as many are doing, competing for Mr so and so but if the mind is weak and uncontrolled, one is ignorant and the ego gets entangled in the five senses. That man becomes a slave to his desires, envy etc etc... What is the purpose of living in this sensual and material aim? Eventually, one will be always miserable and unsatisfied in whatever situation he is living.

The control of the mind depends on its purity. The purer the mind, the easier is it to control. Remember that Purity of the mind must be insisted upon if one wants to control it. Perfect morality is the complete control over mind. The person who is perfectly moral has nothing more to do; he is free and enjoys this life with bliss.

Remember I have mentioned awareness. What I mean is that when one has awareness, one has complete wholeness of LOVE. An ignorant man is a dead body existing only.

"*Loss of awareness is ageing. Absence of awareness is death.*" If one gets control over something, then how can it frighten one? He is the master. If one can learn to view oneself as part of the whole, that whole always remains whole.

Here I mean if one can control one's mind and thought, nothing can act against him in whatever situation he may be!

# CHAPTER 3

# THOUGHT

*There are some people who imagine that some emotional elements or causes or someone else is really responsible for their stress and unless these external circumstances alter, they can never be joyful. It is completely wrong to think like this. It happens that very often people and circumstances around can't be altered, that does not mean that one will stay in stress throughout one's life.*

*Here, it is not the outside circumstances, but one's reactions towards them which cause the distress. One may control one's reactions in such a way that one is not affected emotionally, no matter the situations in the outside world. We have only to detach the mind from the impressions of the external circumstances or divert the mind independently from external situations. If one practices as mentioned, the mind behaves as the master and the external situations become its servant, so that the mind controls the external situations instead of being controlled by them. Hence the major cause of distress and misery is the monkey mind. The external situations act only as a secondary agent.*

*Remember that without the support of mind, no condition or situation can act as a stresser. Anyway, that does not mean that you should not try to alter your external situations for the better. If you have to change your environment for the better, you must do it. After all, a positive environment is a good supporting factor in stress prevention.*

The thought is part and parcel of the mind. If the instrument brain is the head, there must be the mind and the thought altogether. So if the mind is there, the thought as well is there and vice versa. It is crystal clear that without all the three, that is the brain, mind and thought complex, the whole thing such as object and subject as well won't exist. If one however goes beyond these three complexes, then he is free of all attachment and bondage of this material world.

Now attached to the three complexes is another attribute which is the worst enemy of man. This is to let you know that this also is being governed and controlled by the mind or thought. It is a pity that to live in this world, man has to utilize them all and without controlling and becoming the master of them, a man accordingly becomes their slave and it seems very difficult to come out of these above complexes. It demands a lot of spiritual disciplines and practice to go beyond these above mentioned complexes. But really speaking, nothing is impossible and it is only possible with sincerity, regularity and practical method in one's daily life.

However the possibility is that you must turn your thought to some good and positive matter. When good thoughts enter and occupy your mind and heart, they drive away every temptation and evil suggestion.

One should try to focus on the effulgent light which is beyond all sorrows, beyond even the heart that has given up all attachment to the sense objects, or on anything that appears to him as good.

The witness operates at two levels: – objectively as the physical body and subjectively as thought, feelings and emotions. We are meant to operate at this level as one's thoughts and beliefs uphold life in each of our cells. Just as we are an out-cropping of cosmic consciousness, so each one of our thoughts is felt and acted upon by each cell.

Now the important discipline for urgent operations to function smoothly is that the general disciplines for the basic control are practiced. And the utmost and fundamental important thing in the general discipline is the control of thought. The disciple who knows how to regulate his thought, will have awareness of how to control his mind. This is a clue of how to control one's thoughts. Control in an initial stage does not mean that there will be no thought at all in the mind. So here a thoughtless state may be a silly statement. On the contrary in an initial stage thought-control means developing the capacity deliberately to think good thoughts only and to avoid bad or wrong thinking.

One should remember that the only manner to be victorious over the wrong thoughts is to review from time to time the phases of one's mind, to reflect on them, to extirpate all that is evil and to cultivate all that is good.

Remember the teaching of Swami Vivekananda:-

*"We are what our thoughts make us, so take care of what you think. Words are secondary. Thoughts live, they travel far. Each thought we think is tinged with our character, so that for the pure and holy man, even his jest or abuse will have the twist of his own love and purity and do good."*

The most important is the "core of what one thinks". One must set about learning how to practise and do it. That means one must learn how to manufacture good thoughts. In fact, if one wants to produce good thoughts, one must be careful what food one must take, not only through the mouth but through all one's senses. If the food is pure, the thought will definitely be pure. If the food is impure so will the thought be. It is of no use taking wrong food and so making it necessary to struggle to suppress the resultant of wrong thoughts. By all means the thought control does not at all suppress the thought but one becomes the master of it.

In a way, the highest stage of thought-control of course means complete cessation of thought. But as long as one identifies oneself with the ego or the body, one cannot reach this highest stage. This stage is reached by only a handful of fervent disciples in this material world.

The first thing to do is to identify oneself only with God. After practising for a while sincerely and regularly, thoughts will inform their coming, and one shall learn the way they begin and be aware of what one is going to think, just as through a window one can look out and see a person coming. Finally this culmination is only attained when one has learnt to separate oneself from one's mind and see oneself as one and thought as something apart. And don't let the thoughts clutch one, stand aside and they will die out. Be a witness only. Detach and discriminate yourself. And the mind will obey him, who masters it.

This practice is best done of the chosen ideal like in Indian mythology, the "Om."

Be careful that the practitioner be not over zealous to attain cessation of thought without practising the disciplines leading to this highest state. It is better to keep the mind filled with holy thoughts as much as possible, as a result of which the mind will be purified. So when purity of mind is achieved, cessation of thought comes by itself.

The inwardness of thought and concentration are acquired when the mind is controlled. One must think of the (chosen ideal) and know its meaning too. First thing, avoid bad company but keep good company inorder to get good impression. There is nothing holier in this world than to stay in good company, for the good impressions will show on the surface.

To control the mind and senses is the most important feature of the life in the thought stage. It is clear that all the actions and behaviour have their origin in thoughts. The thoughts are not simple things to deal with. Thoughts are powerful instruments with which one can harm others and they should be managed with great care. Although thoughts seem invisible in nature, still they are the powerful forces in this world; without thoughts, the mind won't be able to play its roles in the instrument of human brain.

It is due to the actions of thoughts that the future is being constantly moulded and shaped. To comprehend truly the nature of thoughts and their effects and forces, one must have a well-developed pure soul and mind, and then at this stage they can be controlled to the best of their benefits.

**Vibrations of the thoughts:-** The thoughts as well have vibrations the same as the lights and sound have theirs. When one has good or bad thoughts, the vibrations of these penetrate the environment or atmosphere and influence the persons of the present surrounding positively or negatively depending upon the nature of thoughts. That is why, people must try to have positive thoughts inorder to keep the atmosphere and surrounding clean with any type of evil. "You are what you think." "You are what your thoughts are".

**The different thought and physical vibrations:-** This means that thought vibrations are not the same as physical in nature like the vibrations of sound and light. Thought vibrations are non-physical in nature. The physical vibrations (light and sound) are felt by the conscious mind immediately through our physiology, whereas thought vibrations are first registered in the subconscious mind and from there the impression or urge is transferred to the conscious mind. For this reason, one cannot understand thought vibration so clearly as physical vibrations. Finally, thought vibrations as non-physical vibrations can never be measured by any measurement like physical vibrations.

Remember that materialization also is done through the power of thoughts. The thoughts have great influence on the physical body as well. It is also obvious that the subconscious mind inclines to materialize all the thoughts into the physical equivalent by most direct and practical media available. If the power of thought is very strong, one can have more power of materialization. By reproducing the same thought again and again associated with emotions such as love, faith and expectations, one's inner strength (Gandhi's satyagraha) is enhanced. Eventually, the power of thought increases. If one's thoughts are negative, a negative situation will emanate in life. And if one's thoughts are positive, positive thoughts will manifest out in life. The subconscious mind accepts either good or bad thoughts and it does not differentiate them. The subconscious mind just stores any thought, good or bad forwarded to it by the conscious mind and begins to fulfil it like a straightforward and strong servant of the conscious mind.

However, whatever one thinks, either good or bad, goes on accumulating in the huge reservoir of the subconscious mind. Very often all of us constantly display good or bad impressions according to the thoughts one is nurturing. The reservoir becomes dirty or clean according to what sort of good or bad thoughts are being sent in. So the impressions or urges of these thoughts in the subconscious mind provoke one to have the same thoughts off and in again. Here it becomes a vicious circle which definitely needs to be turned down or rethought.

Now to do so, various processes of yoga disciplines and practises and definite positive thinking are greatly needed here. By doing these practises fervently, the negative impressions or urges of the thoughts can be gradually removed and this leads to the purity of thoughts and of the mind at the same time. Sometimes people treat thoughts as taken for granted; we think that people do not react to our speech and behaviour and nothing will happen just by thinking. But remember that every thought makes a groove in the subconscious mind and becomes part of the overall individuality. Individuality or personality is but a sum total of all urges accumulated in the subconscious mind.

The karmic law is being reacted by harmful thoughts. So by cultivating wrong or evil emotions and feelings such as intolerance, dislikes, hatred, jealousy, revenge etc against anyone, one is actually creating bad Karma as per Karmic philosophy and one will get suitable punishment into the future for this, according to the Karmic law.

Remember that any thought makes a definite impact upon one's future and once it is released, it can't be so easily eradicated from the store of the Karma. It is stored like an abiding record.

Many people think that their thoughts can be hidden. This is not really the case; one may apparently hide one's thoughts from colleagues, friends and give them a twisted version by one's personality, but remember that God who is omniscient watches each and every thought of anyone at moment to moment basis. No matter what happens, nothing is hidden from Him as he is the reality and the spiritual father. He is what is permanent within us, while others are temporary in whatever field.

Everything will be separated from us, one day or the other, except God. So the hidden thoughts can be forecast by telepathy as well. Only when one has awakened one's telepathy faculty can this be done, but without ostentation.

The mind stays immune to negative thought vibrations, only when the thoughts are strong and very positive. What I mean here is that a powerful and pure mind is a definite remedy to any negative thought vibrations or the psychic attacks. The mind when positive has a powerful aura which can't be dominated by any negative thought vibrations. Negative thoughts do not have any effect on such a person with a strong, positive, and pure mind and the bad thoughts rebound without affecting him. To enhance positive and strength of the mind, one must practise yoga, concentration, relaxation and wilful attempt to keep one positive in the daily activities.

Our thoughts captivate some thoughts because the atmosphere is always full of all types of thought vibrations. Whenever one thinks something, one entices the same types of thoughts from the thought atmosphere, the etheric one. And this is done according to this law of psychic attraction. This is like a chain. If one is thinking of negative thoughts, someone will be surprised to see so many other associated negative thoughts wavering in his mind. Likewise when one is thinking something positive, one will be also surprised to see so many positive thoughts and ideas suddenly entering one's mind. So here he can notice how negative thoughts can turn him miserable and down to earth, whereas when positive thoughts enter his mind, these thoughts rise further and further to attain the highest goal in one's daily life. Teilhard de Chardin has remarked, "Tout ce qui monte, converge" (Everything that goes up converges.)

However, bear in mind negative or bad thoughts lower one's mind and make it waver and restless, impure and agitated, whereas positive thoughts energize the mind and make it pure and positive in all fields of activity. It is clear that each type of thought is making a definite impact on our health of the mind as well.

**The Aura**: To create a positive 'Aura' around the body, one must think positively. So the quality of the Aura depends upon the state of one's health and of the mind. Here if the mind is already positive, cheerful and peaceful, the quality of the aura will be definitely very good. (This vibration of aura helps not only somebody but all those who are in contact with him).

The thought vibrations help only when one thinks of something, while one's auric vibrations are always there even when one is not thinking, that is in deep sleep or meditation. So in deep meditation, the aura increases in width. The width of the aura around the body is 1-2 feet, whereas the thought vibrations spread to in larger distances, depending on the intensity of one's thoughts and emotions connected to it.

The quality of aura depends on the character in general and on specific emotions present in the mind at a special time. But the quality of thought vibrations depends only upon the thoughts released at a particular moment.

The aura and thought vibrations constantly influence and modify the atmosphere one lives in or moves about. The aura also gets on being modified depending upon which places and among which persons one usually spends time with. It is clear that if one spends some time in a spiritual atmosphere and among holy and spiritual people, it automatically has a modifying influence on the aura and one becomes a transformed human being.

**Thought Forms:-** Remember that thoughts produce thought forms in everyday life. Meanwhile thought form is again produced in the atmosphere according to what one is imagining and thinking. If one has a powerful and good concentration of thoughts, the thought form will be acute, pointed, clear and pure.

However, if the thoughts are tinged with emotions, the emotional section distorts the thought form either positively or negatively. This is to bear in mind that when one shows anger, hatred, irritation, jealousy etc..., one's thought forms make the atmosphere ugly. If one can detect this as a clairvoyant can do, it looks like a black cloud which looks horrible or even like a hell as well. On the contrary, if one has pure emotions and is positively of love and selflessness', this produces a good atmospheric situation and pleasant thought forms.

The thought form can stay for long and it all depends on the force of the emotions behind it. Remember that the thought form disappears after a limited time and till the energy is drained and worn out. But some powerful and pure thought forms can stay for a long time even after the passing away of the thinker. And anyone approaching these thought forms can feel the impact or influence upon himself.

Now, thoughts can have the same influence of thoughts on others according to the law of thought. The adverse thought forms of jealousy, anger, greed and hatred create same thoughts forms in others who are in his environment. The same happens when a positive, jovial man can pervade the whole environment with happiness by his thoughts which can change even a dark and depressed man into a cheerful one for the time being. Now, a powerful and positive-minded man would not be affected by negative thoughts as a weak-minded man infused with evil, secular and materialistic thoughts is exposed to. That is why we have so many miserable and distressful people with mental disorders of varying degree around us.

Positive thoughts produce relaxation response in the body, whereas negative ones create stress of all sorts in the body and mind complex. Negative mind or thoughts not only agitate the mind, but also produce stress' or violence and hatred (alarm response) in the body; because of this, some biological changes take place in the body system due to the agitation of the (SNS) Sympathetic Nervous System. If this occurs frequently or is one's habit of indulging in negative thoughts, there will be a continuous imbalance in the two components of the Autonomous

Nervous System classified as Sympathetic and Para Sympatric Nervous System and this engenders stress and other psychosomatic illnesses.

Now in Yoga, it is mentioned that when one's mind and thoughts are negatively agitated, the PRANA (vital energy) is upset and consequently the flow of PRANA (vital force) leads to physical disturbances or illnesses because it is clear that this physical body is supported by this PRANA (vital force).

On the contrary, the positive mind or thoughts give relaxation response in the body and bring more physical balance. So when positive Pranic energy is elevated and directed upward in the body, this helps in one's enlightenment, whereas the negative thoughts or mind drain out the Pranic Energy from the body and make the body weak and hinder man from his attainment of his highest goal "Enlightenment".

Finally thought vibrations have influence also on one's physical objects. Remember that the clothes one wears, or the chair one uses to sit on, or even the pen one uses, that is all of them have vibrations. Any one who touches or uses these objects, which one uses frequently, will also take some share of these vibrations and definitely will be infested positively or negatively. And the vibrations also go with the food one cooks or serves, and with all things that one possesses or deals with.

That's why it is recommended in Yoga to stay and work and live only amidst a good environmental and spiritually elevated persons such as Gurus, Sages, etc.. In fact, this is a reason for one to feel so uplifted and purified by touching the objects used or possessed by a great Soul because one can feel the vibrations of that great Soul through that object. This plays a part too when one thinks about a place, one is affected by the thought vibrations of that place as well. If that place and person is good, one will get good vibrations, but if that place or person is bad, one will get bad vibrations. It is said that not only in actions but in thinking as well, one should be staying or living on good things only, otherwise one may be unconsciously doing great harm to oneself.

The process of thought and mind can be modified or adjusted. As I have described, they are the basic nature and laws of thoughts. Now let's go to see how a man should practice in order to ameliorate his thought process. It is possible but not impossible, as there are many methods and ways to control and adjust the thought processes. Here are a few means:

1. The Random and haphazard thoughts. One must try hard to keep away from these random and haphazard thoughts. Make sure that at any time, one's thinking is organized, planned and methodical and not get a habit of random and haphazard thinking. Uncontrolled random thinking and day-dreaming are the results of a weak mind. This shows that instead of controlling one's urges, desires, inclinations and impulses which are stored in the subconscious mind, one is being a slave or controlled by them. The conscious mind has to remain always fully active, in full awareness and keep its master status, controlling its servant, the subconscious mind. If one stays idle, lazy, passive and finally a day-dreamer, one allows the influence of the subconscious mind on one's conscious mind. So make certain that only the thoughts are in one's mind which one really positive at the present moment.

2. Try one's level best to make cautious and wise thoughts stay positive all the time. One must make a cautious attempt in the daily life to observe that everything is carried on positively, even if one is in the most distressed situations. This practice is very useful for as soon as one negative thought enters one's mind, one should convert it into positive one by adjusting again the mental attitude.

3. Try to decrease emotional elements in the thoughts. The emotional elements are likes, dislikes, love, hatred, fear, revenge, jealousy, anger, anxiety etc.. linked to the thoughts which are causing disorder in one's daily life. The major cause of wrong emotional involvement is that people take worldly problems and hardship very seriously in the daily life. It is sure that nothing in this world happens by luck or accident. There is a reason for anything that is occurring to anyone or others. There are many tests and trials that one has to face in this life, according to certain law inscrutable to the discursive mind. Everything that is happening here is for good only, however bad it may look or feel. Actually nothing is planned in a way to harm anybody in this universe. One has to learn certain lessons from all these trials and tests. They are all temporary and will disappear after having served their purpose.

Now, if one takes these trials and tests as a burden in one's life, one is only turning the matter worse and preventing one's release from the problems. However in a spiritual life, someone will realize that he is himself responsible for what is occurring to him. This is a matter of cause and effect law. What one sows, one reaps.

From all these trials and tests of life, try to learn something instead of accusing or blaming so and so. So never lose the balance of the mind and thought in whatever critical situations one is. Be like a spectator or witness of these problems and try the level best to solve them with a detached, discriminate and unprejudiced or neutral thoughts and mind. And nothing on earth can prevent one from one's progress in this only life. See and search solutions for all one's problems. There are solutions definitely if one has a strong and pure mind.

4. One should be faithful, loyal and sincere in one's thoughts, words and deeds. After all, one must have complete faith inwardly and outwardly. Thoughts, words and deeds should be consistent, logical and rational

with one another. A righteous man should have this true test of himself. And in this material world of today, I can say that nearly 99.00% of people have two faces, that's why this world is going to its worst situation. One is the true face and the other is the false one to show to others, what I mean is a double face. One is hypocrite and ignorant and the other to show good they make one feel they are. Finally the inside and outside don't match at all. And this type of duality of character disturbs the balance of thoughts. So the mind of people is sick, they suffer from mental diseases such as paranoia or schiozophrenio, mind is unstable. They become jealous and have envy, lust, anger, hatred and full of desires, which they can't even fulfil; finally, they become big harassment for the family, society and the nation as well.

5. Relaxation of the conscious mind

Be sure that whenever you have time, just go into the practice of conscious mind relaxation. This should be done by shifting awareness of mind from thought processes to pure perception or pure awareness.

The trataka Yoga here is of great help to anyone. One can gaze at the photo of a deity or any other object or better a sacred symbol. Be sure that by simply gazing, there are thoughts involved in it. One will feel tears in the eyes and a burning situation, just close the eyes and visualize the object or deity or photo or flower. If one does get the vision for many seconds, that means that he is doing good. At that level, the mind does not flicker from one to another and one is doing relaxation and concentration at once.

Now, concerning the breathing system, one can concentrate on the breathing system by observing each inhaling and exhaling without making any breathing noise and with the eyes closed. In these above practices of relaxation, the mind is fully active but there is a change of focusing from thought to pure awareness. Remember by practising these Yogic exercises, they stop the restlessness and wavering of the mind and thoughts. Then one can reach clarity and relaxation of the mind. In this state of relaxation, the mind produces relaxation responses in the body and mind complex as well.

Remember that the fundamental thing as a whole discipline is the control of the thought. So one who learns how to control or regulate one's thinking or thought will know how to control the monkey mind. However thought-control in the primary level does not mean that no thought will be in the mind at all. Beware that a thoughtless level may be a silly state of mind. In the first stage, thought-control signifies the developing of the ability intentionally to think of good thinking and to abstain from thinking negative or bad thoughts. Really to vanquish bad thoughts is to remember or recall from time to time the good side of the mind and to reflect on them, and extirpate all that is evil and bad inorder to foster all thoughts that are only good and positive.

Remember the teaching of Swami Vivekananda, "We are what our thoughts make of us, so take care of what you think. Words are secondary. Thoughts live; they travel far. Each thought we think is tinged with our character, so that for the pure and holy man, even his jest or abuse will have the twist of his own love and purity and do good".

These few words (take care of what you think) is the key that one must learn on how to develop it. What I mean here is that one must study how to cultivate good thoughts in one's daily life. One must also be very cautious about the food one eats, not only through the mouth but remember that one must do the same with the five senses as well. As you know, they are the worst enemies of thoughts and mind control. If the food is clean and pure, the thoughts will be pure and good, but if the food is impure, so the thoughts also will be impure and bad.

To have mastery over the mind and thought does not mean that one has to suppress one's thoughts completely. It is useless to consume the wrong food at the same time trying to make it fit to fight to suppress the resultant of wrong or negative thoughts in the mind.

One should turn the thoughts to some good and commendable matter; when good thoughts enter and occupy the heart, they kill away every temptation and evil suggestion.

There is also highest stage of thought-control when there is complete cessation of thought. This is being practised by great Sages. But for the ordinary and common people, this is very difficult. As far as one identifies oneself with the Ego or the body, one cannot attain this highest level.

A Quote from Swami Vivekananda's teaching: "First identify yourself only with God. After a while thoughts will announce their coming, and we shall learn the way they begin and be aware of what we are going to think, just as on the plane we can look out and see a person coming. This stage is reached when we have learnt to separate ourselves from our minds and see ourselves as one and for thought as something apart. Do not let the thoughts grasp you; stand aside and they will die away."

"Follow these holy thoughts of the ideal or Mantra Om etc.. go with them, and when they melt away, you will find the feet of the Omnipotent God. This is the superconscious level, when the idea melts; follow it and melt with it."

One should not, however, be over zealous to reach the cessation of thought, without practising the disciplines leading to this state. It is better to keep the mind filled with holy thoughts as much as possible, as a result of which the mind will be purified. When purity of mind and thought is attained, cessation of thought comes by itself.

This can be practised by anyone, that is to clear the subconscious mind, one has to pour holy thoughts into one's mind and allow them to go deep down within oneself. This is to let you know that holy thoughts are like pure water. The habit of pouring holy thoughts should be done properly and regularly. One must not get worried when one finds the dark water (Bad thoughts) coming out from oneself at a particular level. So if one continues pouring in holy thoughts, a moment will come when one shall find only holy thoughts coming out from one within.

Now the methodical control of thought is an important step in controlling the mind. Don't worry about the future; the present tumbles over. If one is not cautious, one is lured by the present temptations.

By the control of thought and mind, one acquires mental peace. We can do so by simply clarifying our idea and thought of time.

Remember that one of the German spiritual-writers mentions these few words – "In the heart of this moment is eternity;" that means we must clearly see that every moment is only this moment. If one is not seduced by temptation at this moment, one has taken care of one's entire future. By the constant curbing of our evil tendencies, we shall never submit to them.

Therefore in whatever situation, let us stand strong in the resolution of this moment, and one shall really succeed. Therefore the future is nothing but only (Maya). It is foolishness to fear the future while allowing the devil to defeat the present. Spiritual life is really simple, that is to be good in whatever condition, truly moral and to master oneself for only this moment with only purity of thought and mind.

When someone develops love for God, his thoughts and mind dwell on Him, for one naturally concentrates on whatever one loves.

Now to end, there is a procedure to follow in Yoga. One can't just go into meditation without knowing the rules and disciplines of Yoga. One has to follow Hatha Yoga, the eight folds of Yoga. I have clarified these steps of Yoga in other books.

If one follows and does Yoga correctly, then the process of Asanas (postures), Pranayama (breathing), relaxation, concentration and meditation gradually solves all the turbulences of the unconscious mind and turns the mind pure and powerful. Remember that a powerful and strong and pure mind has complete control of its thoughts and doesn't become impure, restless and disturbed as easily as a weak one. So finally, the unconscious or subconscious mind is turned pure by the cleansing of all its bad impulses by powerful meditation; one can also attain the Real Self or Soul or Divine self which is the highest goal in spiritual life; then one reaches the highest source of power, peace and bliss (sat-chit-ananda). That means one has reached the level of the Almighty God superconsciousness. Going from Manhood to Godhood is the ultimate goal of man.

# CHAPTER 4

# AYURVEDA OR AYURVEDIC

This is a Sanskrit word which is found in the Indian Dharma and is used in Indian medicine to signify the entire corps of the medicinal wisdom. Etymologically, the first component of Ayur signifies "Life" and the second part the "Veda" refers to a branch of learning. It is mainly the study of the plants and herbals to relieve man from his diseases which they would have to face during their living in this material world.

Ayurvedic is a Science or art of living as a whole. But the effects are found in the natural plants and herbs, ready to cure people in serious situations when haunted by modern diseases such as hypertension, arteriosclerosis, diabetes, obesity, cardio-vascular problems etc.

It is a science which instructs humans about good living and an art as well by means of which good life is secured and safeguarded. From these two views, Ayurveda or Ayurvedic is helpful both theoretically and practically without any obstruction or deterioration of the body and mind complex.

Ayurveda is one of the main important aspects of Veda, the great Indian Scripture. So the Vedic characteristic of Ayurveda would thus imply the science of life as well as the art of living. According to my experience, Ayurveda can be called the fifth Veda if we regard Ayurveda as an upeveda of Rig Veda and Atharva Veda; the Veda itself is of four parts: Rig, Yajus, Saman and Atharva. So here Ayurvedic is only an (Upanga) or supplementary part of Atharva Veda. Ayurveda was inspired or created by great Sages or Seers of the past and it is still of tremendous importance to all humans to face drastic health situation. These Seers were endowed with extraordinary powers of intuition and vision. Their wisdom and knowledge of human ailments and remedies was perfect; it needs no verification, justification or improvement.

This treasure is amply relevant when we consider how it deals with, food, drinks, bath, anointment, chewing, fumigation etc the major themes.

Ayurvedic is a natural process, for health has always been one of the major preoccupations of mankind. Man's concern with his health is as old as his life on earth. That body should function efficiently was as much a necessity in the early stages of man's existence as it is now. In fact, the necessity then was greater than now for humans then had to be alert enough to cope adequately with the challenges from nature that beset him suddenly, the terrors of the wild and the vagaries of nature were great risks for him. The food that he ate might turn into poison and his bones might break on a hunting spree. Primitive man had to face many hazardous situations. Weakness of the body might greatly handicap him in the perilous and severe race for survival. Finally, the fear of the unknown and the mysterious has always haunted humans from his earliest days till now.

First, according to Ayurvedic as long as man lives in natural life, he is free from many of the ailments that beset him in this luxurious and fake modern world. Leading a fully disciplined life with positiveness is what is wanted.

Secondly, if man's life is no longer natural, then many harmful ailments affect him and they have been plaguing him ever since. So it is clear that diseases affecting mankind have been rampant all the way along. There were periods in man's history when diseases were not so rampant.

"Never was there a time in this world when life was not there, and there never was a situation of life when proper intelligence did not help humans in life goes a saying."

Therefore, in all stages of life on earth, people have been aware of the unfavourable conditions of body and mind complex in life, but also of the means that would cure such unfavourable situations of health.

"Diseases and medicine have always played a part and existed in human and animal life since their creations."

Man's health has always been a preoccupation since time immemorial.

Bear in mind that the fear of death has always haunted man and been the most important motivation for the progress and discovery of techniques to deal with human life. That is the goal of spiritual endeavour as well as all the worldly activities of man have been to prolong life as much as possible. However, religions which believe in life after death and in the immortality of the soul have sprung from this deep-seated longing. The immemorial attempt was to prolong the physical existence itself, to make the body strong enough to survive the odds, to render it in a sense immortal and to transform the essence of the fleeting physical existence into a diamond-like substance. Ref to my book. "Human body is the holy temple of God" to make the body mind complex stronger and purer, inorder to feel God, the Divinity within.

One must follow and have these five practices in daily life:-

1. Food discipline

2. Breathing exercises.

3. Postures (Asanas) for Body Physically

4.  Control of mind and senses, relaxation; concentration and

5.  Purity of love and Sacrifices.

So when your inner Guru is awakened by the help of Yoga and by educing the sleeping (Third Eye) Ajna Chakra which is the inner Guru, then one can find this exterior Guru who will be conferred to him automatically. And once the interior and the exterior Guru come to one's life, then the Divine will be awakened within and finally you become the image of God, then you and Him become One. That is the liberation of man from the bondage of birth and death. (Moksha)

If death do part us creates a great sense of fear; disease is also a major source of concern. After all, it is crystal clear that death is inevitable in this world in whatever fields, either you believe it or not, it has to come, but diseases can be alleviated and get cured from the body. There was a time when the causes of diseases were largely unknown, evil spirits or malevolent deities were sought as causes and black magic, witchcraft and sorcery got importance in human's mind. Even now among materially intelligent people, these above-mentioned evil spirits are still dominant forces in them because they are still ignorant and with weakness of mind. Or maybe, they are still in their subconscious mind from the past birth actions and deeds, which they are still carrying with them in this birth. They should try hard in this human birth to get rid of these fake believes, which lower humans to animalism.

Alchemy – (Rasa Vidiya) was a method that was thus evolved. It was a physical process designed to make the body an efficient instrument both for material prosperity (bheya) and for spiritual upliftment (Uddhara). It is not only religions that have passed through this stage, but even science has gone through it. Medicine especially was in its early phases of development intimately associated with these apparently irrational procedures. It was only recently that medicine was disentangled from this involvement. Long time has gone since Ayurvedic remained stagnant and lay up with primitive beliefs. But nowadays, Ayurvedic is making marvellous progress. Its diagnostic methods, therapeutic procedures, employment of large member of articles most of which are commonly used in the kitchen preparations, discovery of the excellent medicinal properties of herbs, plants, trees and spices and the determination of the dosage and the way of taking medicines are all very well developed, tried out, codified and systematized.

Furthermore, the old ideas of deathlessness, permanence of bodily existence and immunity from all possible forces of disintegration were in Ayurvedic brought down to the idea of sound and effective health.

The Ayurvedic notions of a happy life was not compatible with the liking of the austere, ascetic and puritanical law-givers. They naturally brought forward such advice coming from Ayurvedic sources. "There is no sin in eating meat, in drinking liquor, or in sex indulgence. They are natural indications. But there is great merit in self-restraint"

Ayurvedic looks upon the body as the home of pleasures (Bhoga) and also of diseases (roga).

Moderate drinking can be for enjoyment, it is hearty, it makes one light, is good for all beings, it removes worry, pain and fatigue, it expands the mind and corrects the disorders of phlegm but excessive drinking can be seriously disturbing.

Here Ayurvedic and modern medicine have a great role to play in human life because nowadays there are very few who follow the spiritual rules and disciplines of restraint in once life. One should judge if one is in excess of everything and without control. One must abide by the law of nature in life.

Some time back, health for people was of the highest consideration and proper enjoyment was after all a part of sound health. Clean life, good food, normal pleasures and vigorous health constituted the major part of Ayurvedic ethics; deprivation and over-indulgence were equally wrong in this outlook.

If austerity was prescribed, it was in consideration of health, and not because of religious reasons.

Actually a physician naturally attaches great importance to the body, its preservation and improvement. He is after all expected to understand human constitution and human nature and his job is to secure the efficiency of the physical apparatus that we call this body and mind complex.

In Samkya Yoga and Ayurvedic disciplines, it is considered that the body is something to be vigilant about and to be ruled over with an iron will and disciplined by reduction of demands to the barest minimum.

Phenomenal existence is here regarded not only as unimportant, but as a potential evil.

The outlook that gained currency in the wake of this influence in later period, was that the body was looked upon as essentially an evil, a snare, a home of dirt, a habitation of satanical forces of lust, greed, envy and wrath; by and large, it was considered impossible for the soul to reach salvation until the physical body was eliminated or sufficiently weakened. But Ayurvedic holds the belief that the body is the foundation of all wisdom and the source of all the supreme objectives: dharma (duty), Artha (wealth), Kama (evil), Ahamkar (ego), and Moksha (liberation). Apart from the body, there is nothing that is of help to man here or after. If a man does not realize the (moksha) infinite in this very body, it is even impossible for him to realize it when he has gone beyond the body.

It has found that in later period (Atharva – Veda) itself became Ayurvedic or Ayurveda by focusing its attention on the curative aspect. The diseases which are caused by eating wrong and unwholesome food as nowadays modern common people are used to, can be cured by Ayurvedic treatment, which comes from plants and herbs.

Actually, it is recommended to use Ayurvedic medicine together with working with wind, meaning regulating the breath and suspending it with a yoga technique called (pranayama) and furthermore accompanying it with the body postures (Asana). They don't only preserve this body but make it a glorious one with strong will power. So this glorious body is the necessary precondition for (Salvation or liberation) here and now, in this very body and in this very life. It is in this sense that Alchemy was considered as an adjunct of yoga. If yoga worked with troubles inherent to mind, Alchemy and Ayurvedic dealt with the removal of the natural infirmities of the body. It seems here that Patanjali, the author of Samkya Yoga, the earliest authority on Yoga, can be considered as an alchemist, according to me.

Here I am stressing that besides practising the Science of yoga, the Science of Ayurvedic also must be practised daily as the food one eats is of utmost importance in daily diet.

However, to become a spiritual man, one has to practise the Science of Yoga, that is the eight paths or enfoldment of Yoga, such as:

1. Yama, 2. Niyama, 3. Asanas, 4. Pranayama, 5. Pratyahara, 6. Dharana, 7.Dhyana and 8. Samadhi

2.  Food Control, with the help of Ayurvedic medicine. There is an important chapter on few plants according to my experiences.

3.  Control of Mind and senses should be purified with a pure subconscious mind.

4.  Seek for the purity of LOVE with sacrifice.

5.  Awaken one's own interior Guru, by all the mentioned Sadhanas (Spiritual disciplines) while even living in this material world. One can know his Innerself. As Socrates revealed it (know thyself).

The practice of the above Sadhanas is better carried on with the help of a Spiritual Master. In all the Sastras (Scriptures) the Guru is described to be as good as God, but Guru never says "I am God". The disciple's duty is to offer respect to the Guru just as he offers respect to God, but his Guru never thinks: On my disciples are offering me the same respect they offer to God, therefore I have become God." As soon as he thinks like this, he becomes an ordinary man and may be worst than even an animal. The genuine Guru has conquered his lower self, his ego; so there is no sense of superiority whatsoever.

"The abode of mine is not illumined by the sun or moon nor by electricity, neither by the attachment to this illusionary world of material. One who reaches it never returns to this material world," goes a wise saying.

The Guru's work is to bring his disciples from:

| | |
|---|---|
| Asatoma Sat gamaya | From unreality to reality. |
| Tamaso ma Jyotir gamaya | From darkness to light. |
| Mrityor ma Amritam gamaya | From mortality to immortality. |

In the material world at present, everyone is suffering due to ignorance, just as one contracts a disease out of ignorance. If one does not know hygienic principles, one will not know what will contaminate one. Therefore due to ignorance, there is infection and we suffer form diseases. A criminal may say I did not know the law, but he will not be excused if he commits a murder. Ignorance is no excuse.

Similarly, a child, not knowing that fire burns will touch the fire. The fire does not think. This is a child, and he does not know I will burn him. No there is no excuse. Just as there are laws of the country, there are also stringent laws of nature and these laws will act despite our ignorance of them. If we do something wrong out of ignorance, we must suffer. This is the law, whether the law is a state or a law of nature, we risk suffering if we infringe it. There is a law operating, call it divine, inscrutable to our discursive mind.

"Abandon all varieties of religion and just surrender into ME. I shall deliver you from all sinful reaction. Do not fear," goes another saying.

The Guru is as good as God. When we offer respects to a Guru, we are offering respects to God, because we are trying to be God-conscious; it is required that we learn how to offer respect to God through God's representative.

Then finally one can automatically get the precious chance to get into contact with this exterior Guru. Once this Guru comes in a person's life, he can attain the golden road to the liberation as self-realization or attain the image of God from where we all come from. That is the only Divine path that all humans must tread on; we eventually return to our only father, God. Unfortunately, when humans are born in this world, they also get lost in this illusionary world of materialism. So they are born again and again and get entangled themselves in the net of birth and death.

A very special advice to humans, from my own point of view, please:

1. Stop wondering about the past, what was good or bad in the past. The past is gone, let bygone be bygone. Why harp on them? If not one will be always mentally tired and sick mentally and fragmented.

2. Don't even think about the future which has no sense; example, if tomorrow you suddenly die in an accident, where will be all the future thoughts; all in vain.

3. Don't again and again harp too much about money, money, money. Do you think that the rich people are happy and safe. Never, there have been many examples cited in Scriptures about wealthy slaves.

4. Live and lead a very simple life, use the minimum of these material needs in your life. Don't be like a miser, who accumulates money for any use in his future; when he dies, his thoughts are on them. Discriminate and detach.

5. One must first plan everything with good and pure thinking. And then think clearly and positively and carry on with your action, still with any reaction or any gain only to leave it to Him and never go back for what good or bad, one has done.

Don't remain in the past or the future. These are sins; if one has done a mistake or error, next time try to correct it or don't repeat it again in one's life.

6.  The last and of major fundamental importance in our everyday life: one should always think and remain in the present, I mean now be like a child. He never thinks about past and future. One must have pure mind and thought as a child. If one lives in the past and future, he might live for 100 years and be very rich money-wise with strong well-built body, but he will never be happy. On the contrary, he will be miserable and make all his surroundings miserable and ignorant as himself, living a life of ignorance.

Actually the past is gone and the future is mysterious and unknown. Why make one innocent thought and mind become tired with the past and future events? Give this mind rest; become peaceful and pure; it is all your sincere effort and will-power that are needed and nothing else. And no one can do this for you. You are your own master and failure. It is up to you to decide. Forget the dark side of society, relationship and world affairs. They are here to make your spiritual life a downfall.

What's the use of knowing the whole world when you yourself don't know where you come from, who you are and where you are going in this world? We all need this world but with a life of simplicity.

Take the example of Einstein, the famous scientist who has invented and created the Atomic Bomb for warfare and technological inventions during his life. At the last moment, before death, he finally realized and thought what a great mistake he had done to leave it for the world hereafter. And we can see the worst effect of using the above and the disaster at Heroshima and Nagasaki, it's still vivid in people's mind till now and has been great event in the World War II.

## Now back to the Ayurvedic plants and herbs

Ayurvedic has for thousands and thousands of years recommended plants and herbs for the preservation of health-care and to maintain a positive state of mental and physical health.

Even nowadays, people in any corner of the globe have trusted to traditional Ayurvedic remedies for preventing and treating health disorders or ailments.

Nowadays, owing to the noxious prevalence of pollution in the environment, like smoke, exhaust fumes from vehicles and radiation, chemical reactions take place in our bodies during which electronically unbalanced atoms and molecules are formed. These are called 'free radicals' that affect and weaken our bodies. These radicals are very bad for the body health. They actually attack blood vessels, create memory-loss and hasten senility. They can damage and cause also the manifestation of symptoms of ageing like premature wrinkles.

If free radicals are the enemy to the body, on the other hand, you have then the antioxidants which are the good friends to the body as well. Antioxidants prevent or slow the process of oxidation that does damage, thus delaying the process and harmful consequences of ageing.

Any substance that combats the ill side effects of free radicals is an antioxidant. After all, you must know that the body produces its own antioxidants as endogenous and others are produced by having a good diet as an exogenous antioxidant.

Examples:-

1.  Body-produced endogenous antioxidants are enzymes, co-enzymes and sulphur containing compounds.

2.  The dietary antioxidants produce vitamins A, C and E, corotenoids, bioflavonoids and some sulphur containing compounds mainly the glutathione.

To be free from free radicals, the body needs a balance of the 2 types of body and dietary antioxidants.

Here I have added that apart from Ayurvedic plants and herbs, even a good daily dietary is also of major help to protect the physical body and brain. Mainly all vegetables, green vegetables, all types of pulses and finally without missing all types of fruit.

Before going back to plants and herbs, I am just giving a brief account about our daily nourishment for every human being – inorder to get rid of diseases as I have pointed out.

Actually the body needs a good balance of the food with major antioxidants such as. 1. Carotenoids bioflavonoids, selenium, good fats, proteins, carbohydrates, starch etc.. plus minerals and vitamins to protect the body health.

To have a good and balanced diet, the foods one eats must contain the varieties mentioned below:-

Carrots contain beta- carotene a pro-vitamin. A precursor that improves sight and skin appearance, inhibits cataracts, lung and digestive system infections and may even provide protection from some forms of cancer. Papaya, pumpkin, squashes, melons, sweet potato, berries of all sorts and dark-green leafy vegetables are other sources of corotenoid antioxidants. These capsules of the blue-green microalage, spirulina are rich as well in beta-carotene. Bioflavonoids are the blue and purple fruits like grapes and blueberries and the rinds of citrus fruits.

Generally someone must make certain that his diet contains selenium which is an essential element that helps the liver to function efficiently. To get the benefits of selenium, we have to include whole grains, garlic, nuts and vegetable oils in the diet daily. Citrus fruits, banana, potatoes and wheat grass to get other nutrient based antioxidants such as the vitamins $A, C, B_1, B_5, B_6$, niacin and PABA, the amino acid, cystene, the minerals zinc and selenium and catechols. All these antioxidants are available in almost our daily consumed diet. So problems of diseases happen when any of these antioxidants are deficient in our daily uses and the body has to suffer in any way. So if the body suffers, the mind too will not be stable as they are both interrelated.

This small elaboration of our daily foods is just to give an idea of how the herbs and plants in our daily foods are of great benefits to our body and mind complex.

Now I am going back to Ayurvedic plants and herbs which when used gradually as a supplement to our daily foods will be of still greater benefits to our health. Actually modern science has even approved the therapeutic properties of traditional plants and herbs and brought standard formulations for the health and well-being of millions and millions of people in this modern era.

Plants and herbs have been after all used for healing for hundreds and hundreds of years in many countries and cultures all around the world. Since long, past generations usually knew and respected the natural potency, efficiency and safety of herbs and plants which were tried and tested as remedies for various diseases over years of trial and error.

Even nowadays, either in the West or the East, many of you will no doubt notice a loving grand-mother preparing a concoction or a home-brewed potion of common herbs and plants in the kitchen to sooth a sore throat, heal a wound or ease a pain etc, etc. So here one can define the tradition of using Ayurvedic plants and herbs for healing goes back to at least years and years, B.C. It is very painful and unfortunate to say, however, that with the modern scientific discovery and the advent of synthetic chemicals, human beings' dependence on natural products has begun to diminish with the process of modern pharmaceutical medicines and chemicals. Today, human beings are in favour of pharmaceutical products. It is the fastest remedy that human beings are getting, but they never care about their side-effects which unfortunately follow in the long run. Fortunately in the Science of Ayurvedic, many traditional recipes have been handed down from generation to generation. Very recently the Ayurvedic traditional plants and herbs are being reintroduced to people and are having great effect and concern to human. During the last century, as modern science and clinical trials have begun to endorse the efficacy and safety of these Ayurvedic plants and herbs and their modern day supplements, there has been revival of interest and popularity in natural remedies. Actually, the once declining art of natural treatments has now been revived and come to be acclaimed as a viable alternative to cure a variety of health disorders around the world.

Remember that "UNLESS FREE RADICALS ARE NEUTRALISED, THEY CAN CAUSE GRAVE DAMAGE TO VARIOUS BODY CELLS AND FACILITATE DEGENARATIVE DISEASES." Every single cell of the body is being invaded by "Free Radicals" as many as 10,000 times a day. Much of this damage occurs to genetic material. That is why one needs to keep one's body defences optimised at all times with adequate intake of antioxidants in this modern civilization, else humans will become fragile and weak, as there is great stress in the modern hectic pace of living.

Also to let you know that fruit, leaves, seeds, roots, barks and flowers are very useful to remedy all sorts of cold, cough, sooth, burn and wounds etc, etc..

Now not to go further as there are lots and lots to write about the above same, I am just giving you here a few Ayurvedic plants and herbs which before writing on them, I have personally used as my own experiences for a long time and consequently derive their positive results and remedies :-

They are as follows with elaboration:

1. Aswaganda – (Withania somnifera). The famous Indian plant Stress Buster.

2. Amla – (Emblica officinalis). (The Buster immunity) Indian plant.

3. Ginseng - Panax ginseng and ecenterococcus) Chinese plant for heavy stress.

4. Ginko biloba - (Fountain for the youth and vitality).

   It is used for the circulation of Blood treatment, for memory and other cognitive impairments etc..) and can be found all over the world.

5. Aloe Vera - has a sticky jell in the leaves. Increase (Blood flow, Regenerates cells etc..)

6. Garlic - Comes from the lilaes family as Aloevera. Prevent thrombosis, lower fat and cholesterol in blood and antibiotics as well). Use in the food all over the world.

7. Omega 3 – Polyunsaturated fatty acids. Cure High blood pressure and heart attacks). Come from the fish.

8. Licorice - Glycyrrhiza glabra – Chinese plant. (For cough, Asthma, cold and respiratory illnesses).

9. Honey - Used by all over the world. It has natural vital Energy.

And the rest are such as : 1. Bee pollen, 2. Royal Jelly, propolis, lycium Chinese.

1. ASHWAGANDHA:- Winter cherry or withania somnifera is a shrub which grows extensively in Western India. It belongs to the family solanaceae and has been used as a health food since Vedic times in India.

This root contains a bitter alkaloids somniferi which is the active constituent. It helps to build up energy and vigour in elderly persons, convalescents and those suffering from general weakness and exhaustion. The most efficacious in treating varying symptoms of stress is the herb, Ashwagandha, sometimes known as the Indian Ginseng. Ayurvedic has for thousands of years recommended ashwagandha for preservation of health care and to maintain a positive state of mental and physical health. It has demonstrated its remarkable therapeutic properties as a rejuvenator, fortifier and controller of respiratory disorders as well. Nowadays, modern science has validated those properties Ashwagandha has been found to be particularly useful in health disorders and problems relating to depression, stress and tension. It is also considered as an anti-inflammatory useful in nervous disorders and is a mild analgesic. The major constituents in Ashwagandha are steroidal compounds, their lactories, glycossides and related derivatives, some alkaloids and flavonoids.

Various parts of the above plant contain different constituents. Various heterogeneous alkaloids include cuscohygrine, anatygrine, tropine, pseudotropine, anaferine isopelleterine, 3-tropytigolate, nicotine, withasomine and visamine. (The busk contains large number of amino acids, this tender shoots are rich in crude protein, calcium and phosphorous). It also possesses the coumarin and scopoletin. The roots are reported to have starch reducing sugars, heutriacontaine, dulcitol, glycosides and withaniol.

Clinical researches have demonstrated the remarkable therapeutic properties of Ashwagandha in preventing and addressing cardiovascular and respiratory problems and effects.

Antispasmodic problems - The total alkaloids showed relaxant and antipasmodic effects against several spasmogens on intestine, uterine, bronchial, tracheal and blood vascular muscles.

It is an adaptable plants or herb with many medicinal properties. It is as well used for antibiotic anti-tumour activities anti-inflammatory and arthritic effects, analgesic, antipyretic and anti fatigue.

Ashwagandha is an excellent adaptogenic plants which lifts one when one is tired and relaxes one when one is stressed. It has also good effects on the immune system and energises the human body and mind complex. Most remedies made with Ashwagandha have not shown any undesirable side effects in clinical studies till now; however, some herbs, like foods may not go with everyone. Sometimes a food or a plant may not suit a person, causing diarrhea or nausea, while others may not be affected at all. It happens that sometimes a food does not work well in combination with another food or plant. The caution to be exercised with any remedy, herbal or others is that if it does not suit one or one suspects any problem, discontinue it at once and consult a physician.

This is to remind you that the Ashwagandha is not recommended for people suffering from regular high blood pressure even though it is a good stress reliever.

Finally Ashwagandha takes away the tiredness, ease the tensions and allows one to feel energetic and able to perform well.

2. AMLA:- An antioxidants and the fruits or berries of Amla tree are the richest source of vitamin C. Its botanical name is Embelica of officinalis. This is mostly found in India. Amla is also called in Shanskrit – "Amritphala" which means literally the fruit of heaven or nectar fruit. It has significant quantities of essential minerals like sodium, potassium, calcium, magnesium, iron, phosphorus, chromium, lead, cobalt, nickel, copper, zinc, and cadmium.

The Amla seeds are rich in fatty acids, various enzymes, sugars and tannin. The leaves yield ascorbic acid, inucic acid and gallic acid. Phyllemblin, zeatin, seatin, riboside and aeatin nucleotide are also present in the fruit. The roots yield ellagic acid, quercetin and B sitosterol. The plant contains glycogallin, corilagins, chebulagic acid and diagalloy glucose. There is no adverse side-effects known in Amla. Amla fruit is an astringent, an anti-diarrhoeal, an anti-dysenteric and anti-scorbatic, carminative and a stomachic. Remember that it is also popular ingredient in hair products, laxatives and tonic and remedies for anaemia, jaundice, dyspepsia and urinary problems. It is one of the

94

remarkable herb or plant that finds use in many health formulations is Amla.

Amla is one of the best known among Indian herbs. Time has come when the world would have to recognize its value as the richest natural source of vitamin C and its other important antioxidants. There have been many studies on humans which have demonstrated the positive health benefits of remedies containing Amla such as 1.Anti-diabete activity 2. Upper respiratory tract infection mainly in children.

Everyone requires antioxidants to protect them from free radical damage. Thus everyone young and old, sick or healthy can get benefit from the remarkable antioxidant properties of Amla.

"Amla has amazing properties which boost the body's immunity to stress"

3. GINSENG:- It is a plant form the Aruhaceae family first discovered in China during the Han dynasty (BC206-AD 24) referred to as SHENG. Later it became known as Jen-Sheng, the Root of Heaven.

In 1833 the genus Panax was added to its name Pan meaning all and Axos meaning many health giving properties. Since then, ginseng has been the subject of research all over the world.

Ginseng is considered by some cultures of the Orient as one of the most nutritional herbs as well as one of the most expensive in the world. Its botanical name is Panax Ginseng or Siberian ginseng or Eleyterococcus. The shape of this plants root is similar to that of the human body.

Ginseng is known as a great adapter, that is to say that it helps to normalize functions of the body when a person has been subjected to heavy stress, reacting positively on the nervous and hormonal system.

Moreover, ginseng is of fundamental importance and helpful to the body and mind in various ways:

1. In stimulating physical and mental activity in weak or tired or fatigue patients, which is its most wonderful effects.

2. It also fortifies the human body when it is exposed to severe and prolonged physical exertion.

3. It also greatly helps in the proper functions of the endocrine gland, particularly the hypoplysis, the suprarenal and the sexual glands.

4. Stimulating the nerve cells of the brain, strengthening and correcting some nervous diseases like psychosomatic disturbances, in addition to increasing intellectual activity.

5. No side-effects have been found from taking the famous roots ginseng.

6. A type of ginseng called eleuterococcus was found even in helping in the treatment of cancer.

7. It is also very useful for preventing heart and high blood pressure.

8. It helps in toning the grey matter of the brain, and is a sedative, and also to normalize body functions. It stimulates the production of red and white blood cells, as well as lowering the cholesterol level in the blood in the gastro intestinal; it improves digestive secretions and a great plant for increasing sexual activity.

9. Ginseng also helps to improve memory, improve blood circulation, improve metabolism and restore the nervous

system, normalize glucose levels in the blood circulation as well as improving fertility in men.

Its daily use is of great benefits to the human body and brain. One has to try and experience it. I have tried it and have got the successful results of it in my daily life. Both ashwagandha and ginseng are of great benefits to the human body and mind complex.

4.  GINKO BILOBA: The Ginko Biloba tree is an ancient plant; it is the oldest existing tree species, having coexisted with the old famous animal dinosaurs over 200 million of years ago. Today, thanks to man's intervention, the tree flourishes widely once again growing throughout N.America, Europe and east Asia, China etc..

    Ginko Biloba is truly nature's resilient wonder. It has been demonstrated resistance to temperature extremes, insects, microorganisms, pollution and other environmental toxins. It is called as "Fountain of youth and vitality".

This ancient herbal remedy is that it has the capacity to improve memory and slow the natural mental toll of ageing; it is only the tip of its medicinal iceberg. The cognitive functions reveals that it may also improve the health of blood vessels, alleviate problems with equilibrium and balance, promote the vitality of skin, slow hearing loss, and ringing in the ears and cure some forms of sexual disfunctions, as well as reduce the damaging effects of radiation and ameliorate altitude sickness.

Ginko can be used by adults, young and old ones alike, with potential benefits ranging from improved alertness, attention and memory in individuals to cognitive enhance mating in the elderly, to mild, but potentially important benefits in those with more significant elementary illness.

Ginko combats the free radicals, as free radicals are very high in this modern era. They may be naturally occurring in the body through normal processes, such as those produced by white blood cells in fighting, invading microorganisms and thus have a protective role. Free radicals are also generated in certain disease states and can be absorbed into the body through a variety of exposures, such as inhaling toxins including some pollutants ingesting, harmful foods, including some fats and being exposed to radiation, including sunlights, radiation therapy and nuclear emissions. In such cases, radicals can be quite harmful causing a cascade of events whereby cells are damaged, tissues breakdown, and ultimately cells die. In some case, free radicals generate a chain reaction and cause more damage. One particular target for free radicals are phospholipids, essential constituents of cell membranes and nerve cells including those in the brain. Free radical injury has been implicated in a variety of disease states including AIDS, heart, disease, cancer and the inflammation producing arthritic changes as well as in the physiological changes associated with ageing. This is just an idea what are free radicals.

In Ginko, there is an antioxidant which is called "Flavonoids" which helps to clean up the circulating free radicals and are thus called "Free radical scavengers". These three major flavone glycosides, 1. isorhamnetin, 2. quercetin, 3. kaempferol. The last one is unique to Ginko. Some evidence suggests that Ginko's flavone glycosides may be even more effective antioxidants than either vitamin E or beta-carotene.

The effects of gingko extract have been observed at a variety of cellular levels and on multiple organ systems such as:-

Increases tissue, tolerance to oxygen deprivation, especially in the brain.

Increases blood flow, especially in the microcirculation (e.g the capillaries, where substances are interchanged on a molecular level between the blood and tissues) Enhances the properties of blood that facilitate blood flow. Inhibits the development of grain Swelling or (edema) following trauma or toxic injury hastens its resolution. In the eye reduce retinal swelling and cellular lesions. Facilities compensation in equilibrium disturbances, especially conditions related to microcirculatory problems.

Improves memory performances and learning capacities, prevents cell and tissue damage by scavenging and inactivating toxic oxygen, derived free radicals.

Inhibits the development of age, related decreases in specific neuro-chemical receptors that are sites of attachment in the brain for certain chemicals (muscarinergic, cholinoceptors and a2 – adrenoceptors).

Promotes uptake of a specific neurochemical, choline, involved in the production of phospholipids in the hippocampus, a brain region involved in memory.

Inhibits platelets aggregation and clot formation by antagonizing platelets activating factor.

Protects nerve cells form aschemic injury during periods of insufficient blood flow. A number of other biological effects have been reported but are less well characterized, including inhibition of monoamine oxidase A and B and promotion of glucose uptake and utilization. Further investigation is needed before any conclusions can be drawn about Ginko's clinical utility in these areas but at this time we are unaware of any particular studies underway.

In my experience, ginko is a truly unique compound, really unlike any other natural or synthetic product.

Gingko is truly nature's resilient wonder as I mentioned before. In some ways, it seems to possess the ability to confer this resilience on those who use it.

5. ALOE VERA:- It is a plant that comes from the lilac family, from which garlic is as well a member. But it possesses great curative and nutritive properties such as garlic as well. Its curative and regenerative properties are back dated since the Bible and the ancient Egyptian time. And at that time it was used on bruises and injuries. Now, in modern times, Aloe Vera is being rediscovered and undergone more serious and indepth investigations that assures the effectiveness of its curative properties in various diseases of our modern era.

It has a succulent gel that is obtained from within the leaves, from which it is necessary to remove the peel or skin leaving a slimy, sticky gelatin, like tissue containing tremendous medicinal properties. The principal characteristics that make aloe vera such a marvellous natural product for health and beauty are as follows to:-

1. Pain inhibitor, It reduces pain upon application to the affected area. It has the ability to penetrate very deeply. Aloe Vera blocks pain in the deep layers of skin due to its active components and their power to penetrate and ease inflammation.

2.  Aloe Vera is anti-inflammatory and anti allergic. It works in a way similar to steroids, like cortisone, but without the harmful side-effects. There are several compounds in Aloe Vera. The most important are glycoproteins which inhibit and actually break down Bradykining a major mediator of pain and inflammation. Aloe Vera contains authraquinores salicytatis and magnesium lactate. They are substances that inhibit the histainine reactions made by the immune system in response to irritants.

Don't misunderstand that Aloe Vera contains cortisone but has enzymes and other elements which work extremely well in relieving soreness and bruises in affected areas.

3.  Healing action:-Aloe Vera has a very high levels of calcium and potassium and zinc as well as vitamins C and E. These minerals promote the formation of a net of fibers that trap the red corpuscles of the blood, thus speeding the healing power. And as you know that calcium is a very important element in the proper function of the nervous system and in the use of muscles. And it has a great catalyst in all healing.

4.  Keratolic Action:- This is the action of removing damaged skin, replacing it with new skin cells. It also allows the free flow of blood through the veins and arteries cleaning them of small blood clots.

5.  Antibiotic Action:-

    a.  Antimicrobal activity: It has been proved to stop the destructive action of many bacteria such as salmonella and staphylococcus that produce pus, also combats echerichia coli, streptococcus faicalis as well as being very effective against the fungus candida Albicans etc..

b. Antiviral activity: It fights viruses when used greater than 75% concentration and applied directly to the virus. It is very effective against the vaginal tricomona strain of virus. Acemman acetil, manosa, this substance found in Aloe Vera has been very effective in combating certain virus; it is presently being injected to combat a certain type of leukemia and fibrosarcomas in animals and being studied aid to AZT in fighting the HIV virus (AIDS).

c. Anti-fungal activity, it acts as a fungicide then applied directly to the fungus.

6. Cell Regeneration. It possesses a hormone that accelerates the growth of new cells, also eliminating the old ones. Owing to the presence of calcium in Aloe Vera, which regulates the amount of liquid in the cells, internal and external equilibrium is maintained. This creates healthy cells in all the body tissues. Skin Cancer – Aloe will be a weapon against skin cancer in the future. It also helps to protect the skin's immune system from harm. It contains 17 amino acids which the human body needs for the formation of proteins and tissues. It also contains minerals like calcium, phosphorous, copper, iron, manganese, magnesium, potassium and sodium, essential elements for metabolism and cellular operation.

7. Energizer:- Aloe Vera helps to promote good metabolism, that is the production of energy which the body needs. As it contains vitamin C, it acts to stimulate and improve circulation and the proper function of the cardiovascular system. This vitamin is not produced by the body and therefore one must provide it externally. It is a very important vitamin for the strengthening

of the immune system, circulatory and digestive system and plays a role in the prevention of a vast number of illnesses.

8.  Digestive:- Aleo Vera contains a great number of enzymes. Some enzymes are produced by the body externally. In the process of digestion, the enzymes transform proteins by breaking them down into their amino acids components, carbohydrates into sugar glucose and fats into fatty acids. These transformed elements are then absorbed by the intestine and passed on to the circulatory system. Aleo Vera is used as a laxative and as a gastrointestinal problem.

9.  Detoxification:- Owing to the potassium which it contains, Aloe Vera improves and stimulates the liver and the kidney systems, the principal organs of detoxification. It contains uronic acid which eliminates toxic materials within the cell.

10. Rehydration of skin. Aloe Vera penetrates deeply and restores lost liquids. It also helps in repairing damaged tissue from the inside out, burns and sunburns.

11. Nutritional:- Aloe Vera is a mystery plant which contains nearly 18 of the 23 amino acids that the body needs to form cell and tissue. It also has enzymes necessary in breaking down carbohydrates, fats and proteins in the stomach and intestine.

    N.B. Aloe Vera contains a large variety of Vitamins like $B_1$, $B_5$, $B_6$, $B_{12}$, A and C. And also contains minerals such as calcium, Phosphorous, Copper, Iron, Magnasium, Maganese, Potassium and Sodium.

12. Natural cleanser as well, because it contains sapomins as well. It is a natural cleanser due to the oil it contains. Owing to the

presence of proteolitics enzymes, it destroys dead tissues, thus cleaning wounds.

13. Fights irritations: It eliminates burning and itching and very useful for bites and rashes etc..

14. Dilates vessels:- It dilates the capillaries thus, increasing blood circulation.

15. Great transportation inside the body. Owing to the presence of lignin, Aloe Vera penetrates and is the perfect transport or distributor of other elements with which it is combined deep inside the skin.

16. Aloe Vera is also useful in Dentistry, toothpaste made from Aloe Vera helps to combat bleeding and gengivitis in the gum, and prevents tooth decay without the abrasive action which prolonged use causes tooth decay itself.

17. Aloe Vera in Beauty Care. Aloe Vera has become a tradition in beauty care as being an important element in many types of beauty products. This is to remind you that Nefetiti and Cleopatra used Aloe Vera for their beauty treatments. It has two components. Lignin (cellulose) and polysaccharide (carbohydrates) which truly penetrate the three layers of skin, the epidermis, the dermis and the hypodermis and clean out bacteria and oil or grease deposited that block the pores. It is used in moisturizing creams, night creams, masks, shampoos, toning creams and facial cleansing creams etc.. It is also used in suntan and other skin protection lotions cream. Aloe Vera is also used in cream for muscular and rheumatic pain and stiffness as well as in gelatine form it helps to combat acne.

Finally Aloe Vera has no known side effects till now. Any one young, middle and old ages can use it in any given ways.

6. GARLIC: It comes from the same family of lilac as Aloe Vera. Garlic like as Aloe Vera has medicinal properties; garlic is characterized as possessing a buried stem in place of a root. It is rich in sugars, proteins, calcium, potassium, phosphorous, sulfur, iodine and silicone. And also rich in vitamins $A_1$, $B_1$, $B_2$, $B_3$, and C. Garlic contains allicin, a powerful natural antibiotic in many cases stronger than penicillin and tetracycline Garlic has always been famous in medicinal uses since antiquity. The Babylonians used it as a miracle plant in 3000 BC. Nowadays also garlic is an Antibiotic for cough suppressant, Anthelmintic (against intestinal worms). Antirheumatic, fight hyperthyroidism, Muscle relaxant, Aids digestion. Diuretic, Anti diabetic, fights hypertension, Heart relaxant. Garlic prevents alteriosclerosis, thrombosis, lower fat and cholesterol in the blood and general revitilizer and reconstructor. Garlic has been used as condiment in foods as giving taste or flavour. But it has its great curable effects on human diseases such as:-

a. Antibiotic and germicidal power, it has been greatly demonstrated against bacteria like staphylococus, streptococcus, salmonelle, and other germs that cause diarrheoa and gastrointestinal and bronchiopulmonary infections. It also helps in the case caused by fungi like ringworm and candidiasis.

b. Lung Decongesant. It acts as a great lung dicongestant helping to loosen the harmful infections secretion of bronchial tubes.

c. Killer of parasitic worm. Since ancient times, garlic's gloves have been used to get rid of oxyuriasis (intestinal worms) in children and eleminate amoebas.

d. Antirheumatic, Rubbing ground garlic mixed with hot Aloe Vera lotion calms and eases pain caused by inflamed and aching joints a result of rheumatism.

e. Hyperthyroidism. It contains a lot of iodine which helps people who suffer from hyperthyroid, a deficiency of this mineral.

f. Muscle Toner, Muscles can be toned by taking garlic, which then can sustain an extra amount of work, as the Egyptians, who build the great pyramids have said. After all it is a great muscle relaxant.

g. Digestive: By using garlic, it prevents the blockage of gastric, pancreatic and intestinal juices, which are responsible for digesting the nutrients by nerves or stress. It also promotes a relaxed and toned digestive system:

h. Diuretic:- It is highly diuretic due to its essential oils and its low molecular weight sugars.

i. Anti-Diabetic: It has a big help to people with diabetes because it lowers the level of glucose in the blood. This is due to the fact that it increases the secretion of insulin, insulin; is in change of maintaining normal levels of sugar in the blood.

j. Hypertension : It lowers high blood pressure, garlic acts as a vasodilator which helps to widen blood vessels, making blood flow smoother. This helps in lowering blood pressure.

k.  Heart relaxant: garlic regulates the cardiac rhythm, helping to avoid arrhythmia. This is beneficial for people that have accelerated heart rates and cardiac arrhythmia.

l.  Reduces fat in the blood. Garlic promotes a decrease of low density in lipoproteins . It lowers the cholesterol and triglycerid. It works miraculously by reducing in levels of detrimental cholesterol (LDL) as well as an increase in beneficial cholesterol (HDL) when a little garlic is given daily to patients.

m.  Arteriosclerosis and Thrombosis Researchers from different institutions presented their studies in which the positive influence of garlic was determined in the prevention of Arteriosclerosis. And that it diminishes coagulation and the destruction of clots in blood circulation.

n.  Revitalizor, since time immemorial, garlic has been associated with vigor, physical strength and force and promoting great strength in athletes. Everyone can use it, mainly the middle and old age people.

7.  OMEGA 3: Our modern researches have found that the daily uses of a group of polyunsaturated fatty acids called Omega provides great healthy benefits, principally to the cardiovascular system. It helps to prevent problems of the cardiac and circulatory systems like arteriosclerosis, highblood pressure, heart attacks and embolism. One of the principal fatty acids is Omega 3 (Liloleic acid) as will as Omega 9 (Oleic-acid) which along with Omega 3 have wonderful therapeutic properties. After all it has been found that Eskimos and fishermen who eat a large amount of fish have fewer heart problems, fewer problems with diabetes, high blood

pressure and cases of cancer than people whose diet contains a high consumption of red meat. A mix of these fatty acid, omega 3 and 9 gives a highly efficient combination for the reduction of cholesterol and triglycerides, improving general health. They may lower blood pressure, a major risk factor for heart attacks and stroke and reduce the tendency for blood platelets to stick together which can lead to formation of blood clots. They may help repair the damage due to a lack of oxygen in body tissues. Omega 3-9 help to reduce the risk of cardiovascular problems because it reduces cholesterol in the blood. It also helps in avoiding the risk of deposits of cholesterol in the arterial walls. Reduce the level of triglycerides in the blood that is fats that are strongly implicated in obesity and heart attacks, strokes. It reduces the risk of Thrombosis. Helps to normalize blood pressure, also causes symptoms of premenstrual syndrome. Shows the advance of multiple sclerosis, and the effects from the consumption of alcholic beverages. The growth of cancerous tumors are slowed. Increases the mobility of blood cells. Helps to avoid blood clots as mentioned above, making platelets less sticky. Prevents the development of rheumatoid arthritis and finally helps to combat skin diseases like psoriasis and eczema. Thanks to all the researchers who make our lives easy, but people must follow their fruitful advice for their health.

8. LICORICE:- Licorice is well-known for its sweetening characteristic. The roots have tremendous therapeutic properties and has been used by the Chinese for more than 5,000 years. It is called sweet root, because it is sweeter from 50 to 100 times more than the table sugar.

It has innumerable virtues as medicinal uses. They use it for gastric and duodenal Ulcer treatment. Licorice deglycyrrhizinated) is very effective in helping people who drink alcohol, coffee, take aspirin or other medications which irritate the stomach.

It is after-all a great remedy for cough, asthma, colds and respiratory illnesses. Owing to the licorice's ability to stimulate the immune system by inducing the production of interferon the body can defend itself against viral infections, as well as combat the presence of bacteria. It has been used for thousand of years to fight respiratory illnesses such as cough, bronchitis and colds.

1.  Antiallergenic and anti-inflammatory: Licorice has antiallergic and anti inflammatory properties, probably due to the fact that it acts on tissues in much the same way as cortisone but without the negative side-effects.

2.  Herpes complex: Owing to the stimulating effects of this herb on the production interferon. Its effectiveness has been proven when applied to the affectes by herpes.

3.  Hepatitis and cirrhosis of the liver: Licorice has a beneficial effects on the liver and has been proven not only by stimulating its functions and detoxifying it, but by directly treating the ulcers.

4.  Arthritis: Owing to its powerful anti-inflammatory properties, it is used with great efficiency in the treatment of this illness.

5.  Premenstrual Syndrome: Licorice neutralizes the irregular syndrome by means of its artiestrogenie capacity and its ability to prevent the decomposition of progesterone into another molecule.

Licorice should be taken under a treatment by a Doctor is preferable. It is not recommended for hypertension or kidney problems.

9. HONEY:- Honey is a natural vital energy, which has been taken from the nectar of flowers which are impregnated by the sun's rays. It is a wonderful source of food and a tonic. In Ayurvedic, honey is a natural, living food-stuff. Since the beginning of time, man has been fascinated by the bee from which honey has been taken. Actually bees produce honey, pollen and propolis. As a general rule germs don't grow in pure honey. For this purpose, honey has been used in the past to nourish babies and the sick.

Honey contains an ample amount of nutrients such as; caracternoids that are converted into vitamin A, Vitamins $B_1$, $B_2$, $B_3$, $B_5$, $B_6$, $B_{12}$ Biotin and Folic Acid, Calcium, Copper, Iron, Manganese, Phosphorous, Potassium, Sulfur and 19 amino acids, including

8 essential ones, with varions enzymes and carbohydrates.

According to Ayurvedic, honey is natural, living food-stuff. It has wonderful properties for revitalizing the human body. At birth, the baby should have his tongue coated with honey, his first food. Pure honey never gets spoiled if kept clean for years & years.

Honey and soaked almonds may be used against mental sluggishness, for it is a powerful tonic for the brain, a dozen almonds are soaked in warm water overnight and in the morning the skins are removed. The almonds are eaten with two spoon of honey. Within few days, one will feel full of energy and life. Remember that a teaspoon of honey a day will keep the stomach and bowels in good condition for the rest of our lives.

N.B. People often by misunderstanding say that honey is fattening. In fact, the contrary is true for in ancient times it was used not only to regenerate the body but also to slim it. Honey is recommended during a slimming diet because it is very quickly absorbed, unlike other sugars which are "metabolized" much more slowly thus causing undesirable fat to accumulate in the tissues. This is why honey when taken in small quantities, is not only a wonderful health food, but enables one to stay slim.

Finally, I have given a summary of what I have myself experienced in this human form.

After all, the mind is everything. If one wants either to make this world which is after all an illusion as a real hell of his own, it is up to him. Or if he wants to make this same world a Paradise, it is still up to his own free will; both exist within the human being, who is a rare, special and extraordinary species in this universe. This rarity is not found in animals or plants.

Everyone has to decide his own real way of living if he wants to come out from this circle of birth and death. This human form is a gift from God. No one can help you to attain whatever field you decide. You are your own destiny and fate; you can even go higher than fate and destiny or out of it. It is all his own decision in this only human form.

Your right decisions and right actions are yours; it is up to you to make the best of this human life by practising the Science of Yoga. That is the only way to reach our goal as we are images of God and finally we must all return to Him, our final abode in this life or next.

# CHAPTER 5

# LOGIC OF AYURVEDIC IDEOLOGY

*The impact of good food on man's mind is of the mendous importance. The proper foods in right proportions are useful for keeping good health in the body; they also give a definite power to the human mind. Everything that human consumes produces a sensation on the sense palate, that is the tongue as well as certain chemical effects on the body and brain. After all, it is quite clear that the feelings created by the food determine specific mentality. 1. Meat-eater produces gross material reactions that develop the material or animal mental tendencies, 2. whereas by eating raw vegetables and fruit, this helps to reinforce and develop the good (Satwic) quality of the spiritual in human himself.*

According to Ayurvedic, there are the positive and negative qualities of food. Since Ayurvedic deals with holy and spiritual way to healing of body and mind complex, it has always treated the diet aspect in very proper way and depth for our own benefit in the health domain.

Ayurvedic has classified personality traits into three different parts, based on the food which human consumes:-

1. The Satwic or spiritual quality food for spiritual growth; but very few people in the material world are thus.

2. Rajastic, an active quality food for common and ordinary people who are involved in half material world.

3. Tamasic, a material quality food for complete material people who have no discipline at all on foods.

112

Remember that the mind is affected by the quality foods one eats.

1. Satwic food can be digested easily and brings balance to one's mind. By eating Satwick food, it helps in building immunity and ameliorating the healing power in people who are not well. Satwic food is all pure food which is mostly from nature, in the natural form and which most spiritual followers uses such as milk, milk products, fruit most fresh vegetables except (garlic, onion, scallion and clives). Grains cereals like most lentils, sprouts and natural sweeteners like jaggery, honey, natural oils like ghee, butter and vegetable oil.

This is to let you know that Satwic food is cooked moderately with the adding of few spices and less fat. Black pepper and chillies are never put in cooking. But some common spices like turmeric, ginger, cinamon, coriander, aniseed and cardamon are used in satwic cooking. Actually raw foods are not advisable in Satwic, as they contain a lot of microbes and germs. According to Ayurvedic, raw foods are known to weaken the digestive system and diminish the (ojas) which is synonymous with vital energy also known as Prana (life force). The ojas sakti is very useful for the proper functioning of the mind and for the spiritual development. However, a spiritual man who depends on the Satwic food habit is known to have a clear mind with a good balance, with moderation in habits and with clear focus or forecast about any good work, actions and thoughts. He usually stays away from intoxicants like alcohol, stimulant like tea, coffee, tobacco and non-vegetarian food. A Satwic man is also supposed to be of spiritual awareness.

2. Rajastic food is heavy to digest, but it can be fresh. This food is for those involved in heavy work or physical activity. He is a non-vegetarian food eater like meat, fish eggs, chicken, pulses and grains which are not spouted. The foods are being prepared with sour, salty,

spicy ingredients which increases Rajasic qualities. Under this category hot spices, pepper, chillies, vegetables, with onion, garlic are included.

It contains spices and oil-cooking even freshly cooked with high quality of nutrients. This food is of great sensual stimulation and the man of rajistic food is usually aggressive in nature with quarrelsome energetic disposition. He is only interested in power, prestige, position, prosperity with name and fame. He is heartless and love to enjoy material objects at his maximum. His mind is confused and fragmented; he becomes very selfish and also ignorantly indifferent. Such people are the most miserable but they show the feeling that they are the happiest people in this fake and illusionary world.

3. Tamasic foods are not fresh and are unnatural, overcooked, stale and processed. Tamasic foods are made from refined flour, pastries, pizzas, burgers, chocolates, soft drinks, stimulants like, tea, coffee, tobacco, intoxicants like alcohol and wines. The canned and preserved foods like jams, jellies, pickles and fermented food are under this category. The fried foods, sweets made from sugar, ice creams, pudding and most modern junk foods, spicy, salty, sweet and fatty food are also classified under this heading. Actually Tamasic means darkness. The man with tamasic character suffers from intense mood swings, insecurities, desires, cravings and is unable to deal with others in a balanced way. Tamasic man has little regards for the welfare of others and tends to be very selfish and self-centred and full of ego. His heart and nervous system does not function normally; such man ages very fast and usually suffers from degenerative conditions like cancer, heart disease, diabetes, arthritis, chronic fatigue and with all sorts of mental and bodily problems in his daily life. Tamasic man has no control over his appetites and indulges in mindless eating.

Rajasic and Tamasic man would benefit from switching from Rajasic and tamasic diet to a satwic one.

Satwic food elevates man to spiritual way of life, whereas Rajasic food leads man to materialism, selfish way of life and the worst is Tamasic food which degenerates man to a devilish and animal way of life.

It is very sad to say that people in this modern world are becoming completely tamasic; they are self-centred, neurotic and ailing; they are reaching a point of no return. This kind of tamasic food has become an epitome of modern and fashionable way of living and which is of unhealthy nature. Ignorantly the new generations are leaving the wisdom of Satwic food, which is very deplorable and they are moving fast towards the diseases of an unhealthy tamasic food. And how do you want that our society won't be degenerating into violent, self-seeking people, hungry after power and uncaring?

Now just a hint and idea about your digestive system. First it takes roughly 13 hours to digest the raw vegetables, fruit sprouts and while cooked vegetables and pulses take about 24 hours before your system is able to absorb them. And remember that it takes 72 hours to digest the non-vegetarian and fried foods. It is due to our intestines inside which measures about 22 feet (7 metres) the small intestine and the large intestine is bout 5 feet (1.5 metres) long. Altogether they measure about 27 feet (8.5 metres). Actually the food is divided into four natures, cold, hot, warm and cool in line with their actions of curative effects. The foods of cold and cool temperature can be used to treat hot-natured diseases, whereas hot or warm foods can be treated for cold-natured diseases and finally some foods are neutral in nature.

1.  Here is a list of cold and cool foods in nature: barkley, millet, buckwheat, green bean, coixseed, celery, spinach, lettuce, green

cabbage, stems, turnips mainly white, bamboo shoot, lily bult, lotus root, eggplants, tomato, water melon, white gourde, sponge gourd, cucumber, bitter melon, apple, pear, orange, banana, rabbit's meat, duck's meat, duck's egg, crab, fresh water snail, kelp, green tea, soy sauce, table salt, rock candy etc.

2. Hot and warm foods in nature: glutinous rice, cheese Sorghum, pumpkin, hot pepper, ginger, scallion, onion, leek, funnel green, garlic, parsley, mustard greens, dates, walnut kernel, plum, arbutus, pomegrenate, longan, peach, cherry, apricot, chestnut, pineapple, spirit, vinegar, black tea, pepper, coffee, chicken, turkey, mutton, venison, spotted silver carp, grass fish, trout and red sugar, etc.

3. Neutral foods in nature: Polished rice, wheat, corn, soyabean, pea, small red bean, cabbage, cauliflower, carrot, fungus, silver fungus, muchrooms, yam, day-lilly buds, peanut, potato, lemon, grapes, cherry apple, olive, lotus seed, pork, beef, spring chicken, pigeons meat, quail's meat, egg, carp, mandarin fish, eel, turtle, jelly-fish, abalone, white sugar, honey, jasmine tea, wulong tea etc..

This above description is just a clue of your daily foods and in which nature they are classified.

Here there are five kinds of taste of food, which are as follows:

1. Pungent kind or flavour taste are:-

Ginger, scallion, garlic, hot pepper, pepper, ayenne pepper, onion, leek, spirit, few of these foods are used to treat common cold,.

2. Sweet kind or flavour taste are potato, lotus root, wheat, polished rice, peas, milk, chestnut, date and honey. Few of these foods are used to treat weakness and deficiency.

3. Sour kind or flavour taste are lemon, grape, papaya, cherry apple, pomegranate, tomato, tangerine, plum and vinegar; few of these foods are used to stop diarrhoea.

4. Bitter kind or flavour taste are bitter melon, almond, lily bulb, orange peel, tea, coffee, bitter green, arrowroot and pig liver. Few of these foods are useful in febrile diseases treatment.

5. Salty kind or flavour taste are barley, millet, dried purple sea weed, kelp, jelly fish. pork, beef, crab and table salt. Few of these foods are also helpful for some treatment as well.

Now, just to awaken you consciously that man has been created as a vegetarian and is borne out by the molars that are designed to crush and grind. The Saliva is alkaline in nature, which is perfect to digest plant protein. The stomach and the greater length of intestines are designed for vegetarian food as referred above. The liver of human beings is also not equipped to get rid of excess uric acid that the animal protein breakdown produces. Owing to eating animal, gout which is a painful disease is being spread to human.

Vegetarian diet is considered be of great benefits in my own experience. After all, vegetarian diets are lower than non-vegetarian diets in complete fat, saturated fat, and cholesterol. These factors have an incidence upon high risk of obesity, coronary, heart disease, high blood pressure, diabetes mellitus, and some forms of cancer. Logically, it is clear that vegetarian foods are healthy and nutritionally adequate when appropriately organized.

It is also clear that vegetarians have a lower average of blood cholesterol, therefore a reduction in the risk of coronary artery diseases, obesity and less digestive problems compared to non-vegetarians.

Plant foods have shown to have a chemo-preventive properties which protect man from all these above mentioned diseases. The risk of breast, prostate and other cancers is substantially lower in those who consume vegetarian aliments.

Here are added some recommended facts of vegetarian foods:-

1. Vegetarian foods of any type should include a wide range of foods and enough calories to meet one's energy needs.

2. Keep one's intake of sweets and fatty foods to a minimum because those foods are lower in good nutrients.

3. Consume whole or unrefined grain products whenever possible with fortified or enriched cereal products.

4. Consume a lot of variety of fruit and vegetables, which are good sources of vitamins.

5. Wherever milk is the main source, please choose skim or low fat or non-fat milk.

However, a daily diet should be a balanced one to keep the body and mind complex strong enough to face the daily work and hectic life of this modern world. Man should think about the involution of his own welfare in his life, which is considered to be a must in this hustle and bustle world. Evolution is good, but without involution it is not a balanced and well equipped living inorder to face this polluted environment, which man himself has created due to his ignorant and selfish way of living.

It is high time that man reacts to it. Remember that medical scientists have produced medicines of all types to heal man against all sorts of diseases, but medication has got heavy side-effects on human body and mind; the medicines are mere palliatives but in the long term these medicines have great side effects on humans. But remember that in our forefathers' time, the sages used herbs, plants and all types of foods for curing all sorts of diseases but without any side effects. By recent research done, Ayurvedic plants, herbs and even foods are being rehabilitated with a great good effect in this modern era. From the last century pharmaceutical drugs, people have forgotten much of the rich heritage of the medicinal uses of plants, herbs and specially the foods. So to avoid the side effects of drugs, the attention was diverted to alternative Ayurvedic and food cures. Since the last two decades, scientists and Ayurvedic world widely have found that the real medicines that could bring relief to man in most diseases can be found in their everyday consuming of right foods in right proportions and in plants as well as in herbs, which were discovered by our fore-farthers and sages from time immemorial.

Nowadays, with new health-information from food diets, Ayurvedic and Science, one can definitely control one's own health. Gradually, by making changes in one's dietary habits, one may prevent and alleviate both chronic and acute ailments from one's own mind and body complex. Many modern types of diseases such as infectious, cardio-vascular diseases, high blood pressure, cancer, gastrointestinal diseases like ulcers, arthritis, skin disorders, headaches, weak energy, constipation and insomnia of these modern ailments can be minimized or even eliminated by consuming the pure kind of food daily.

Actually, food has an unbelievable range of substances which covers natural laxatives, tranquillisers, beta blockers, antibiotics, anticoagulants, antidepressants, painkillers, cholesterol reducers, anti-inflammatory agents, hypotensives, analgesics, decongestants, digestive expectorants, anti motion sickness agents, cancer inhibitors, antioxidants, contraceptives, vasodilators and vaso constrictors, anti cavity agents, anti cavity agents, anti ulcerative agents, insulin regulators etc, etc. There are after all medicinal compounds in variety of foods that can match with the recent medicine invention or drugs of this modern time and can work wonders. Anyway, there are food items which have been used by generations before, but no one has paid any such attention to the natural aspects of these foods which cured ailments from time immemorial. Nowadays, researchers have found interest again in the healing powers of such foods which have stunned modern scientists. It is surprising to let you know that there are about ten thousand of plytochemical substances that exist in all the variety of foods we do consume everyday, mainly in vegetables and fruit. These plyto-chemicals give the plants their normal colour and flavour, and also serve as the plants defence system against disease and pollutants. Meanwhile, they protect consumers against a lot of illnesses prevalent in the modern frenetic lifestyle.

Here, I am not going into deep details about food protentialities in one's life. But a short list of the beneficial power of foods and fruit are follows:-

1. Apple:-

A good medicine for heart patients. It lowers the blood cholesterol (mainly the green one) and lowers the blood pressure. It stabilizes the blood sugar. Apple juice immunized the infectious viruses. It also moderates the appetite, and finally it has a lot of chemicals that block cancer.

2. Banana and Plantain:- They prevent and heal ulcers and lower blood cholesterol.

3. Fig:- It helps to fight cancer; the juice helps to kill bacteria, round worm and helps digestion.

4. Grape:- It helps inactivate viruses, thwarts the tooth decay and it is rich in substances that block cancer.

5. Lemon and Lime:- They prevent and cure scurvy and contain chemicals that also block cancer.

6. Orange:- Helps to combat certain viruses and lowers the blood cholesterol. It fights arterial plaque and lowers the risk of certain cancers.

Short list of foods which have healing powers as well:-

1. Barley: It lowers blood cholesterol, may also inhibit cancer, can improve bowel functions and relieves constipation.

2. Beans:- Such as black bean, black eyed peas, chickpeas, faba beans, kidney beans, lentils, lima beans, split peas, white and navy beans, common baked beans. They reduce bad type blood cholesterol and contain chemicals that inhibit cancer. Control insulines and bloodsugar and lower blood pressure, also regulate functions of the color.

3. Cabbage:- It lowers the risk of cancer, especially of the colon. And also it prevents and heals ulcers mainly when consuming the juice. It helps in stimulating the immune system by killing bacteria and viruses and it fosters growth in human body.

4. Carrot:- Lowers blood cholesterol and prevents constipation and very useful for cancer and lung mainly for those who smoke.

5. Cauliflower reduces risk of cancer of colon and stomach.

6. Brinjal or Obergine:- In protecting arteries form cholesterol damage; has chemicals that prevent convulsion.

7. Garlic:- It helps to fight infections and has chemicals to prevent cancer. It makes the blood thin mainly anti-coagulant. It also reduces blood pressure, cholesterol and triglycerides. Stimulates the immune system. It also prevents and relieves chronic bronchitis. It also acts as a decongestant and expectorant.

8. Ginger:- Prevents motion sickness and makes the blood thin and lowers blood cholesterol as well.

9. Green Chillies:- Good for the lungs. Act as well as all expectorant and prevent and alleviate chronic bronchitis and emphysema and act as a decongestant and help to dissolve blood clots and kill pain.

10. Mushroom helps to thin blood, lower blood cholesterol, stimulate the immune system and inactivate viruses.

11. Onion:- A multi-faceted heart blood medicine. It helps to boost beneficial HDL cholesterol, good for the blood and retards blood clotting, regulates blood sugar and helps in killing bacteria.

12. Pea:- highly in contraceptive agents and rich in compounds that prevent cancer. Prevents appendices and helps to lower the cholesterol.

13. Rice:- Lowers blood pressure, fights diarrhea, prevents stone in kidney, clears the skin disease and partly contains chemical to prevent cancer.

14. Soyabean:- very good for cardiovascular and lowers the blood cholesterol meanwhile prevents and dissolves gallstones. It also reduces triglycerides. Regulates the bowel and removes constipation and regulates blood sugar and lowers the risk of cancer and promotes contraception.

15. Wheat Bran:- relieves constipation, prevents diverticular disease, varicose veins, haemorrhoids and hernia.

16. Yoghurt:- kills bacteria and prevents and treats intestinal infections, including diarrhoea, lowers blood cholesterol, boosts immune system and improves blood functioning and prevents ulcers and has substances for anti-cancer.

17. Seaweed or kelp:- They help in killing bacteria and boost the immune system, healer of ulcer also reduce blood cholesterol and lower blood pressure, thin the blood and prevent strokes.

18. Olive oil: reduces bad LDL and raises good HDL and helps in thinning the blood and contains substances to retard cancer and ageing, also lowers risk of death in all causes and as well lowers blood pressure.

19. Oats: very excellent for heart, lower blood cholesterol and regulate blood sugar, combat inflammation of skin and act as a laxative.

20. Nuts:- very good for energy and strength which have good cholesterol HDL and very good for brain and memory as well.

21. Honey:- used as an antibiotic and kills bacteria, also used as a disinfectant for wounds and sores, reduces perception of pain, also alleviates asthma and soothes sore throats, calms the nerves, induces sleep and finally relieves diarrhoea.

22. Milk:- prevents osteoporosis, fights infections especially diarrhoea, modifies upset stomach from harsh foods and drugs. Prevents peptic ulcers and also cavities, chronic bronchitis. It increases mental energy and lowers high blood pressure and blood cholesterol and inhibits certain cancers.

As vegetables, there are others such as beet, celery, parsley, radish and spinaches, tomatoes, broccoli and etc.. which are very much important in our daily food requirements to keep us in a healthy situation. As fruit, there are others such as Blueberry, Cranberry, Cherry, Grapefruit, pomegranate, mango and all sorts of berries, orange, papaya (paw-paw), peach, pineapple, dates, raisins and apricots etc. Before I end here, I have to mention one important tea, green tea, which is a mystery if used in our daily life. Green tea protects blood vessels, suppresses cancer and prolongs life. In recent years, it has been proved as a mystery combatant against free radical damage since it has a value and a quantity of antioxidant. It has a chemical substance such as catechin and is known to lower cholesterol levels and diminishes blood clotting.

Before ending this chapter, who doesn't want to look younger, maybe 10 to 15 years than the real age? Please don't expect miracles overnight. But be patient and make practical disciplines in these rules which will get you to the highest destination about your health which is really precious as gold to each one.

1. While getting up in the morning, take a glass of cold or warm water first thing or a glass of fruit juice.

2. Drink a glass of vegetable juice every day. Raw vegetable juice is full of known and unknown antioxidants. These help to reduce free radical activity.

3. Try at least to use four serving of fruit and vegetables daily. One cannot estimate the value of fruit and vegetables.

4. Use less oil in cooking. If excess fat is used, this increases free radical activity. These free radicals are in excess of what the body can normally diffuse and cause ageing in man. Remember that recycling the used oil is a harmful habit practised in most households in their cooking.

5. The green tea works wonders in one's life really. Remember that the Chinese or Japanese eat a lot of fish and seafood and drink

a lot of green tea. If you want the same benefits, do switch to green tea at least as it has a lot of antioxidants in it.

6. The worst thing that our modern world is used to is the refined of all flour, sugar, rice etc. People should stop it and go to unrefined foods.

7. Stop smoking as it can make people look old by ten to fifteen years apart from playing havoc on their health. Undoubtedly it ages the skin and brings wrinkles around the face and eyes.

8. The stomach should be kept ¼ empty. This helps the digestive system to function correctly. One must eat at least two foods rich of calcium everyday. It can be a bowl of low fat curd and some soya bean or bowl of (channa) gram soaked in water right before. Curd plays an important role in the gastro-intestine track and is healthy to the bones. Soya bean also maintains healthy bones and has innumerable health benefits.

9. A brisk walk for 30 minutes regularly for at least 5 days a week. Very good to relax the body and mind complex.

10. Always keep a positive outlook and thinking.

11. To keep the mind busy and strong positively, always keep involved in family and friends and do everything with love, sacrifice, discrimination and detachment, with a sense of belonging, work as shock absorbers and help rev up the immunity system.

12. Do thing and action that makes you really happy and free. Also do meaningful work as duty and with honesty and live one's life in a conscientious, responsible way, this brings inner peace and longevity.

The above daily disciplines, one can use them as the 12 commandments in one's daily life to reach the ultimate goal.

N.B :- There are two types of proteins, animal protein and vegetable protein:

1. Animal protein can be found in meat, fish, egg and all dairy products.

2. Vegetable protein is found in grains, beans, pulses, nuts, seeds and sprouted seeds.

3. This third is a special one which is found in fish called Omega 3 Fatty acid. This is very beneficial for depression. Decosahexaenoico acid (DHA) is the building block of human brain tissues. Lower levels of DHA have been associated with depression. Food sources leading to Omega 3 fatty acids include walnuts, salmon, trout and tuna.

Vegetarians can consume lot of walnut in their daily life inorder to get access to Omega 3 to fortify their brain tissues and to be safe from depression.

*Hunger is not an occasion to enjoy food. Since no one can avoid it, offer some food to the body, when it is suffering from pangs of hunger, while the body is ill, treat it and bring it back to normal health by consuming satwick food, Ayurvedic plants and herbs and by the practice of Science of Yoga. Every one suffers chronically from this regular discomfort called hunger. The remedy for it is food; thus eat food as a medicine, not for greediness, enjoyment and pleasure but for the relief from the pains of hunger. The food must be offered to the Lord in devotion and with silent prayers before taking it as communion.*

# CHAPTER 6

# MENTAL PROBLEMS

In this chapter, I have thought very deeply and want now to deliver the goods to the people of this era, who are missing a lot in their lives. So here I have mainly prepared these few chapters especially to those who are suffering and to protect those who have not yet been beset by distressful situations, which are very crucial in one's life.

My main idea is that people should not get sick unduly, but owing to the material pressures and the modern hectic pace of living, they are physically and mentally in bad shape. There is a solution to it, if they can spend at least half an hour of their precious time daily in performing Yoga. It is a matter of practice, not only reading and following this theory only. I stress again on the regular practice which is of vital importance. Just start it and after a while you will judge if I am wrong or right. It is an individual performance with true sincerity and determination. Your body and mind are yours; it is up to you to make it a temple of God or a derelict house.

**Mental Troubles:-**

There are many external and internal situations which make the mind harshly strained and in the end it loses its balance. Gradually, its performance gets disturbed and its peace starts to get agitated, either slowly or quickly, all depending on the mental health and state of the individual. If someone is so affected for a long time, he becomes a mentally sick one, with varying degrees of mental disorders. Finally the individual's action, thought, deed, manner, behaviour and physical outlook become unbalanced and various forms and shapes or abnormality are being involved. There is no boundary for such mental problems; any person of whatever race, age or any sex and of any socio-economic standard, from any place and area can be affected by them.

Here two types of disturbances and sickness are being mentioned, they are :-

1. How to ameliorate and remedy the case of mental sickness.

2. How one can keep a sound mental health.

Both answers are found in the system of the Science of Yoga.

The reasons of mental problems which affect the individual come from three basic sources:

1. Nature, 2. Society, and 3. Self-individuality. In other words, the major problems that strain and cause mental unbalance in each individual are nature oriented, society oriented and self-oriented in one's daily life.

Truly speaking, first troubles might arise out of nature and can be in the forms of some natural calamity, danger from certain animate creatures and the curiosity of natural events.

Second, the social troubles can emanate from socio-religious, ethnic, racial, economic, political and so on. And this might involve various problems of adjustment to some customs, manners and behaviours and ways of life of a different community.

Third, there can be large amount of problems in the individual's own imagination and creation, which originate from certain wrong habits, manners, beliefs, faults, notions and especially from some inside feelings and emotions such as desire, jealousy, revenge, intolerance, hatred, adulterous inclinations, romance, envy, lust, wrong likes and dislikes, sorrow and happiness etc, etc.

Remember that this world has been always like this since time immemorial. Man of every culture, whatever the background, industrial agrarian, tribal, or primitive has always been faced with such various troubles based on these three above-mentioned sources. No matter the changes in nature and forms of human problems in their social situations, fundamentally they have remained the same. But there have always been solutions to all these above problems. And these solutions have been introduced spiritually to either the ancient or modern world. It is up to the individual to realize his own innerself; then one can face such problems and life becomes a reality of pure love to live in.

Here, the steps of yoga are the only essentials for obtaining the desired goal in both levels, either physically or mentally.

These steps of Yoga are eight. And now a brief implications with meaning are mentioned below:-

1. Yama :- Control and discipline.

2. Niyama :- rules, methods and principles.

3. Asanas:- Practising body postures.

4. Prayanamas:- (System of breathing – Kriyas).

5. Pratyahara:- Avoidance of undesirables in taking actions, that is, knowing the proper actions.

6. Dharana :- Concentration.

7. Dhayana :- Meditation.

8. Samadhi :- Contemplation and transcendental.

Now to make it easier to the disciples or aspirants, these steps are being grouped under different Yoga according to their nature and substance. If one reads and practises Geeta, the Mahabharath of Lord Krishna, one will definitely have a good understanding of practising them in one's daily life, like Arjun as a disciple who followed Lord Krishna as his only Guru.

The Yoga that covers these eight steps are the following four:-

1.  Jnana Yoga :- Yama and Niyama and is the Science of acquiring proper knowledge.

2.  Hatha Yoga:- Asanas and Prayanamas and is the Science of Physical excellence.

3.  Karma Yoga :- Pratyahara and is the Science of action.

4.  Raja Yoga :- Dharana, Dhyana and Samadhi, and is the Science of concentration and meditation.

And finally you have one more Yoga very particular; this one is Bhakti Yoga. This is a Science of Pure Love. Love others as you love yourself. Then you and God become one and only one. There are many examples in the Scriptures.

**To practise Yoga:**

Those who are going to practise Yoga must have the mental ability to understand its basic principles, methods and thoughts and are physically in a good condition to perform even the simplest postures or practices. Make sure that these basic requirements about the mental and physical are executed, if not, it would be difficult for one concerned to make proper use of Yoga. So here the practitioner should definitely go and read chapter one inorder to understand the discipline of Yoga. With a brief understanding of the first chapter, they can begin practising Hatha Yoga step by steps.

Hatha Yoga consists of Asanas, Pranayamas, bandhas and mudras. There are some selected items and postures initially. These are specially for mental problems. When they feel alright and recover, they can proceed to other items as well according to their liking.

One should begin his practice as follows:-

**First Week:**

1. Ujjayee Pranayama in lying position.

2. Suryanamaskara. (salutation of the sun)

3. Uthanpada Asana.

After these postures, one should rest in

4. Shavasana – Which means dead corpse for about at lest five minutes.

One can refer to any Yoga book.

**Second week and third week.** During second week they should add the following Asanas:-

5. Paschimotan Asana.

6. Bhujanga Asana.

7. Trikona Asana.

Repeat Shavasana for Ten minutes after.

**Fourth Week.**

Gradually add either all the Asanas given below or they should choose and practise only those which they can perform comfortably:-

8. Sarvangasana Asana.

9. Matsya Asana.

10. Dhanur Asana.

11. Hala Asana.

Repeat the Sharasana for ten to fifteen minutes at the end always.

RAJA YOGA: - Mental concentration.

The first primary step of Raja Yoga is the concentration and this is meant for common and ordinary people of this material world. But there is another advance stage which is meant for higher spiritual people and this does not mean that it is impossible for others. It is possible if the higher Yoga practices are being followed with strict rules and disciplines in one's daily life. Now if the will of the individual is strong, he can concentrate with one-pointedness of the mind.

As you have read on the mind control chapter, you might understand it clearly. If one has this strong will-power and a strong mind, one becomes skilful of mind control and can control with facilities its fluctuations and vacillatious. And the mind is not permitted to run out and attach itself to numerous issues, thoughts, events and objects. So at that stage, the mind becomes very selective and for some desirable reason.

Remember when the maximum concentration is reached through good and regular practice daily and with sincerity, it has great creative effects upon the problems of mental illness. Naturally, mind always tries to associate itself with some events, issues, objects and thought. The involvement is with only one thing at a time, though the duration may for a short while or longer one. Finally to what it will attach itself none can predict.

The connective nature of the mind creates specific situation in the body and this should be understood.

As mentioned above in the nature of the objects, issues, thoughts, events and so on with which the mind attaches itself, so it has the same reaction in the body. In Yoga, it is said that unless distraction of the mind is controlled and its energy is clearly channeled towards the desired purpose, nothing worth naming can be accomplished by the individual. In the end, the capacity to control the mind and canalize it in the proper direction is reached through the perfect training in concentration.

And the concentration exercise and practice also is being described in chapter of mind control. The method of practicing this sort of concentration is named TRATAKA.

**Some cautious measures:-**

The followers must be very careful. As in any other Science, the rules of Raja Yoga should be continuously followed inorder to avoid undesirable results. And nothing serious will befall one if guided from a Master; always remember these:-

1. The limitation of time not more than ten to fifteen minutes in a session with twenty-four hours unless guided by a Master. The limitation is for good reasons.

2. If the followers do practise for getting thrills and fascination, then he is not only diverting himself from the desired goal,

but also taking himself to some unknown consequences which might have ill-effects on his actions, thoughts, performances and behaviour.

**Checking the Level of Concentration:**

When practising, you see the shape of the actual object through the inner eye even for a second, that means you have gained concentration. But when the concentration on the object remains before the Inner-eyes of the eyebrows, (Ajna Chackra) in any form or shape, for up to five seconds, you have got good concentrating, further more if one can hold the image for up to ten seconds, one has got a very high level of concentration. Finally when one has reached higher level of concentration, one mental illness or disorders must have already been wiped out and one has completely returned to a normal life.

Finally it is up to the individual himself, no one can do this for him. What is needed is not only theory, but all depends on how regularly and quickly one is practising daily. Nothing is hard if practice is done.

God, the Almighty be with you all who follow the practice without failures or excuses.

Peace be with you all.

**To relieve or release from the Root cause of Tension.**

There are 10 Rules or guidelines to reinforce the pattern and attitude of mental conditioning. You must have the capacity to remove the contents of the mind that create so much havoc in your lives Anyone can change his mental programme or at least modify it by removing all the dross or unwanted parts. What is needed, is the desire to reorientate your life along new paths, ways and to translate this desire into personal effort.

After all, the choice is yours. You can either take responsibility to make this world a veritable heaven on earth here itself or you can remain as you are, that is in the same rut of materialistic way of worldly living.

These are only to overcome daily tension in one's daily life. And only practice them as you go in person your daily routine and their presence will help you from within, the subconscious centers. One has to practice daily these 10 guides given below.

**The 10 rules and guidelines are as follows:-**

1. Insist on the effort and begin to accept other people fully. If you can accept others more, they in turn will start to accept you too.

2. Someone must accept himself as he is. Accept your limitations. Meanwhile feel the need to clean out the mind of its conflicts; it is your inability to accept yourselves that causes so much anguish in your life.

3. Be very careful about your behavioural and habituated reactions to other people around you and to your environment. Try to reduce your need to find happiness in outside things. And if in anyway, you don't get what you want then accept it with a shrug of the shoulders, with a sense of detachment .

4. Search for your greatest needs, attachments, desires etc… Be as decisive and critical as you can. To find out your attachments is to go deep into the cause of your present anger or your present sorrow back to its root and there you will get the emotional and mental attitude that causes the agitation or inconvenience. See how you respond with people whom you dislike or not getting on well with . These people will help you to know and remove your emotional attitudes.

Remember that the world and its people are only as your teachers in whatever situation you are.

5. As far as possible, live in the present (now). Don't worry about the past and what has already happened or by harping on pleasurable past features. And again don't anticipate the future.

One can make plans, but planning as being part of the now, and not as really being to the future. If one wants to live life to the fullest, one must try to live each moment, each present moment as completely as possible by bringing one's attention to the (now). Whatever work or action one does, try not to think of its consequences good or bad; do it disinterestedly as enjoined in the <u>Gita</u>. Enjoy every work and action at any time and moment.

6. Never identify yourself wholly with your actions, your body and your mind. Nearly all people identify themselves wholly with their minds and bodies it is the false ego. They ignore the consciousness that lies behind everything they do. When the purification of mind and body is done, they will see and identify themselves with this underlying consciousness.

7. One should try to be more frank and open to people and manifest true and honest feelings as far as possible. Always remember that when you try to be what you are not, then you try to impress or influence people and when you hide your inner feelings from others, you immediately experience mental stress and alienation. This tends to intensify the feelings of "ME AGAINST THE WORLD". And even the most insensitive person can detect to a degree if you are trying to hide something, or if you have a guilty secret, for one might be hiding or have hidden the same type of guilty secret.

8. Bear in mind that all of you have the potential to reach the highest levels of awareness in this human form. Man's present attitude towards his environment or towards anyone is caused by mental programming. But when he starts to understand himself and his mind, his mode of living which is temporary will change and become more harmonious. Most people have an unrealized potential in just awaiting to be tapped. Finally see this potential in everyone, no matter how difficult it may be.

9. Face all difficult situations with equanimity and try not to avoid them. Actually one builds one's life so that one interact with people one dislikes as little as possible. And one tries to associate oneself with people and situations which tune in with one's emotional programming. And as such one continues to live in a way that reinforces and satisfies one's prejudices. One should treat difficult circumstances and animosities as the great teachers. It is after all they who can show most clearly the way in which our mental programme works. It is the enemies who bring to the surface our emotional conflicts and prejudices. It is after all very few people who are really aware of programming and conditioning. Once this is recognized, then one can start to deal with it.

10. Try and put oneself in other people' places instead of blindly reacting in ways that you are programmed, try to look for the other persons' point of view. If someone gets vexed against you, try to discriminate and understand his manner and character in this situation. If is also your programming to become angry when someone vexes at you. Remember the reaction is purely automatic. Try to change your response so that the

140

vexed situation does not cause emotional upset in you. Finally cultivate this detached habit in other situation in your life.

The root cause of tension or stress lies in the mind. The cause lies with conflicts and fears which are submerged in the subconscious mind and whose nature one is not aware of. All one feels is the tension and emotional upsets that manifest in one's live. One often experiences the results without knowing the source of the problem. The unhappiness and tension is a certainty, but the reason is an uncertainty.

In my experience, there is only one process of eliminating these subconscious impressions which make life miserable for much of the time. This process is to be aware and know the mind. One has to explore one's own mind and come face to face with these subconscious mental impressions. This process demands both effort and time. However, many people cannot even consider exploring and knowing their own mind because first this demands physical and mental relaxation. This is very important so that one can disentangle one's awareness from the outer environment and petty problems and direct it inwards. Therefore, many people have so many problems that their awareness is completely involved in worries and outside distractions.

So here relaxation is the door to health, happiness and lighter consciousness. A few minutes of conscious relaxation can help one to remould one's life pattern along more effective and harmonious directions.

# CHAPTER 7

# HEART ILLNESSES AND HIGH BLOOD PRESSURE

People suffer from the illnesses of the heart and blood vessels, called the cardiovascular diseases. Actually, owing to our uncontrolled way of eating rich foods, these diseases have become the main killer in all developing countries. And it is, as you can see, cardiovascular disease is a frightening epidemic of this century.

However, it is of fundamental importance for the sufferers to know 1. What the Cardiovascular Diseases are? 2. What causes them? and 3. How these Cardiovascular Diseases can be controlled, cured and prevented by a Yoga therapeutic practice. But some basic understanding of our organs seems to be important.

The organ heart is a strong muscular pump whose regular function is to pump blood to the arterial system at an average rate of 70 to 80 times per minute. The heart keeps the blood circulation going on by receiving it in its chambers from all parts of the body through the veinous system, and then pumping it out to all parts of the body through the arteries. It is a complex organ and which can be damaged at any time in an individual life span. If the circulatory system does not receive the needed supply of blood, this defect can be in the heart itself or in other parts, such as the lungs, kidneys, the brain and other organs. A damage or breakdown in the heart can become heart-ailment or heart-attack as people usually call it.

Here the cardiovascular diseases which can be treated by therapeutic of Yoga are the following:-

1. Arteriosclerosis – (stiffening of arteries)

2. Coronary thrombosis (sudden blocking of the arteries of the heart)

3. Degeneration heart disease.

4. Hypertension diseases.

**A brief explanation of these diseases are being given below:-**

1. Arteriosclerosis – heart disease

Here the inner walls of the entries get thickened due to gradual deposits of fatty material. This fatty material takes the form of layers in the inner walls of the arteries causing an obstacle to the flowing of blood. Gradually, the blood clotting covers in the rough areas and the blood circulation is hampered.

2. Coronary Thrombosis – heart disease

This occurs when an immediate block of one of the arteries or its branches happens, then the supply of blood to the heart is obstructed partly or wholly. This happens due to the deposit of clot in an already narrow-artery. Owing to lack of blood supply, a heart attack takes place with chronic chest and arms pain and there may be perspiration through the whole body.

3. Degenerative Heart disease:-

This occurs when there is a frequent decay of the blood vessels. It is due to excessive smoking of cigarettes or drinking too much alcohol in any form; it causes degeneration of the blood vessels. It frequently happens among the middle-aged and the elderly people. In this case, the heart does not have enough strength to maintain the needed healthy function.

4. Hypersensive Heart disease:-

This happens owing to constant presence of high blood pressure in the individual. If the blood pressure goes up and stays on a very high level, it makes the heart muscles and the circulation system overstrained. So, this overstraining causes wear and tear of the tissues, leading to the stiffening of the vessels, and reduces the supply of blood to the heart and brain.

It happens that the supply of blood to the brain gets so diminished that paralysis of one or both sides of the body occurs. A major cause of cardiovascular ailments is due to psychosomatic factors. The disease resulting from strain and stress is known as psychosomatic, Psyche and Soma, (which means mind and body).

However the most common strain and stress is due to nervousness, which occurs because of fear, anxiety, apprehension, tension and restlessness, anger, jealously, frustration and many different feelings in the human mind.

According to Yoga, the mind controls, activates and governs the body and its organs. So the body is an instrument of the mind; what happens is that the mind straining factors begin to strain also the bodily system. Nowadays, most of the diseases such as heart ailments, hypertension, and others are mostly related to our mental strain and stress which are called in medical term. (psychosomatic factors)

What is H.B.P. in human body:-

A normal blood pressure in a man stays 120 systolic and 80 diastolic. Owing to abnormalities in the arteries or in the circulatory system, the systolic pressure rises high and same-time the diastolic also goes up. Bear in mind that the rise in the pressure occurs due to narrowness in the arteries, the heart has to work harder for pushing the blood through them and as a result of which, there is high blood pressure, and this is called hypertension. When blood pressure continues to remain excessively high, it causes various disorders as lack of strength, tiredness, headache; and at times, difficulty in breathing, bad temper, visionary troubles, and coldness in the hands and feet. In medical term, hypertension may be due to psychosomatic factors as mentioned above or it can be due to advancing age and thereby to degenerative factors as well.

Treatment possible :-

Nowadays, there are medical treatment for them as well as in Yoga. Remember that Therapeutic Yoga should be practised when the person concerned is not affected by an emergency type of condition. Experiences have shown that due to Yoga practices, the patient of heart ailments have come to their normal health within two to three months. And once the restoration of health has been achieved, the patients stay in good health without any complaint. And even in cases of high blood pressure, a patient becomes normal as well within one to two months, if he/she has been co-operative in following out practices and instructions. Finally the treatment is of three sorts:-

1.  Observance of certain principles and advice.

2.  Eating habits – proper diet.

3.  Practising Yoga on a selected basis.

The main advice is that patient should stop smoking cigarettes in any form, and give up tea and coffee. Alcoholic drinks should be stopped. Eating of ghee, butter, cream, eggs, meat, excessive fat containing in food items must be stopped as well.

N.B. Hot spices, pickles, chutney, red chillies and excessive use of salt should be excluded from eating foods. Should avoid over eating at the times. Must also stop late hour working and keeping awake longer during night. If such precautions are taken, this will definitely prevent the ailments of heart.

Read the first chapter of this book for advice and a diet chart is annexed on obesity chapter.

The main advice to everyone is that people should be relaxed and keep themselves from anxiety, nervousness, tension and restlessness.

It is hard for every one to be relaxed in all situation and conditions, but it can be done with right understanding about the SELF, SOCIETY and NATURE, which have been discussed earlier in Mental problems chapter. The readers are advised to read them clearly for their development of self-power to face these tensions which create all types of troubles and problems.

**A guidelines of Yoga are given below:-**

First part:- For 3 weeks.

This should be carried on for three weeks. Only Shavasana needs to be followed and practised. Before practising, the practitioner should first read and develop a clear understanding about this process of Shavasana. Practise it in a very slow method, not in a hurry and with great patience and be quite at ease.

Daily practice is of utmost importance.

Shavasana should be practised three times daily if possible. It should be practised for 20 to 30 minutes daily at one stretch. Suitable times to do it are in the morning before breakfast, in the afternoon 2 hours after lunch and in the evening. Remember that the stomach must be empty while performing it. After three weeks when checked that the blood pressure returns to normal, then people should add asanas which will be the 2nd and third part. If the blood pressure is more than 150 systolic, they should keep on practising only Shavasana till normal systolic comes back. Experiences have shown that remarkable good effects are achieved by patients of heart and high blood pressure if regular and proper practice of Shavasana is done. Shavasana improves the disorders of the circulatory system by relaxing the nerves and the internal organs. So when normalizing and relaxing effect on the arteries highblood pressure is diminished, it is gradually remedied.

SHAVASANA PRACTICE:-

Six main steps are here described:-

1. First lie down on your back. Keep the whole body loose, easy and in a straight posture. Palm can be down on the floor and facing upwards. No pillow should be used. Keep breathing in normal way. And also keep the eyes closed and let the whole body fall on the floor without strain. This is the position to get ready and this stays during actual practise till the end.

2. Close the eyes and keep them closed for two seconds. Then open them for two seconds and do this simple opening and closing of the eyes for three to four times.

3. Open the eyes again and look upward, then downward, then straight. Now look towards the left side, then towards the right side, the straight again and then close the eyes. Do this eye exercise up to three times.

4. Now open the mouth wide without straining it. Turn the tongue inside the mouth in such a way that its tip is folded back towards the throat area or palate then close the mouth. Keep the mouth closed and tongue folded for 10 seconds. Then open the mouth and bring the tongue back to its normal position, then close the mouth. Repeat for three times.

5. Keep your eyes closed and bring your mental attention towards your toes. See mentally that the toes are relaxed. Then move slowly upward and towards the head area mentally by checking

the knees, thighs, waist, spinal cord, back, shoulders, neck, arms, palms, fingers and rest of the areas of the body to be sure that they are actually relaxed. (Make a slight movement of the neck and head by turning right or left) not so important. The whole mind body complex must rest at a comfortable position and mainly the body is physically relaxed.

6.  Then relax the mind with the following process. Select a place of natural beauty which you have ever visited and liked, such as a park, garden, a lake or a river-side and feel as if you are mentally present at that place. Attach your mind to that place without any dual thinking. Feel as if you are lying at that place and breathing the air of the same environment. Now while keeping the mind involved with that environment, do some deep breathing. In this deep breathing, just exhale and inhale slowly but deeply. During breathing the stomach should go upward while inhaling and it should come downward while exhaling. One exhaling and one inhalation make one round. Do not rush in this deep breathing. Make about ten to twelve rounds. When the deep breathing is over, feel as if you are going to sleep. Now relax completely and stay in that position for five to ten minutes. Then open your eyes and stretch your body and then be seated. The Shavasana is completed.

Practise Shavasana always at the end of Asanas, Pranayamas, Mudras and other Kriyas and should be done for 10 to 15 minutes. For people who suffer from insomnia, high and low blood pressure, gastric troubles, lungs and heart troubles and mental suckness, Shivasana is a remarkable Kriya for immediate relief. Those who feel lack of energy, tiredness, fatigue and lack of vitality will find this asana as a giver of energy and strength.

N.B. If this Shavasana is coupled with Ujjayee, this is a fantastic Yoga and Pranayama boost up of vital force nergy in humans either physically or mentally.

There are various practices of Shavasana. All depends on the Guru's instructions. They are all formidable to practitioners.

2nd part for forth and fifth week:

When the first part is completed for 3 weeks, then the following asanas can be added as from 4th week. The asanas are as follows:-

1. Pawan muktaasana

Do it with one leg first right and left as after with both legs. Make 3 to 4 rounds daily.

2. Uttan-Padaasana: with only the leg at a time, hold for a few seconds and then to six seconds 3 rounds of each leg or one can do with both legs up to 4 to 6 seconds.

3. Shavasana : Should done at the end for 10 to 15 minutes as described above.

Third part (Six week onwards)

The daily practice of Yoga should be in the following order:-

1. Pranayama – with Rachaka and puraka.

2. Suryanamaskara asana.

3. Santulanasana.

4. Pawanmuktasana.

5. Uttanpadasana

6. Shavasana – as describe before.

This is the end of this heart and blood pressure problems. It is hoped one who practises these Yoga will be overcome sufferings by the grace and blessing of the Almighty when awakened within with courage, perseverance, sincerity, and regularity. The goal is achieved surely.

Shavasana: for non believer of religion as well. It should be practised with the word "relax" which is also in a form of a Mantra.

# CHAPTER 8

# OBESITY OR OVER WEIGHT

Over-weight is one of the modern common health risks, because millions of people, in both sexes and of every age are suffering from extra weight on their bodies. People with overweight are alarming and frightening aspect because it shortens the life span and causes arteriosclerosis, coronary heart troubles, hypertension with high blood pressure and various physical and also mental psychosomatic ailments and disorders, and makes the life of people miserable due to complications such as diabetes, indigestion, gastrointestinal disorders, sexual incapacitation and inferiority complex.

However, to understand the problems related to obesity, overweight is not obesity. Over-weight means carrying a few pounds of extra weight than the body frame requires. If a grown-up man of average height carries five to ten pounds of extra weight, that means he is overweight but not obese.

In women, the fat generally accumulates in the hip area and in the thighs. In men, the fat accumulations in mostly the abdominal part and less in other areas. But in most chronic cases of obesity, this accumulation of fat and muscle covers the whole body.

## Origin of Obesity

However, it is very difficult to say the exact cause of obesity. But one can say that it is a consequence of too much eating. There are other factors also involved in it, but really speaking one thing which is certain is that without excessive eating generally, there would not be obesity.

Obese people easily develop some common habits, make some common mistakes and they all have the common characteristics in their daily life.

1. People have become addicted to over eating.

2. No control or discipline in eating habits. They eat most of the time.

3. The habits of eating faster and without chewing the food properly.

4. As soon they have finished dinner, they get to bed immediately.

5. Or sometimes, they do not get time or purposely avoid to do physical exercises.

Nowadays, obesity is due to the result of our modern civilization. The monotony of everyday life is that man gets up in the morning, has his tea on the bed, then gets up and shaves, washes up, dresses up and has a sumptuous breakfast, comes down in the elevator, gets to his car, rides to his office building, takes the elevator upstairs, sits in his chair for office work, goes downstairs in an elevator to the restaurant in the same building, has his lunch, and comes back to his office and sits then till the closing of the office, and then takes his car and back home. When at home, the same routine again during evening, he watches T.V while drinking beer or other drinks, then has dinner of best food and plenty of drinks and soon retires to bed and goes to sleep. This routine and habits are being followed everyday in his life. So imagine what is going to happen to the body and mental complex with such above explained routines. Man is bringing his own downfall about his health and finally overweight, obese and obesity becomes the trigger or target to man's ailments, where all sorts of chronic diseases would definitely infest man's body after a while.

Now the most harmful problem related to obesity is that one develops a sort of inferiority complex in one's daily life. He wants to cut off from friends and social groups. He builds up a secluded life. And he feels that he needs an isolation or in company of his own type and he develops bad habits, such as taking alcoholic drinks, using intoxicating drugs and adopting all sorts of harmful ways of living. Eventually, he develops all sorts of mental disorders, as nervousness, tension, anxiety, fear, lack of confidence and he is entangled in a sort of vicious circle. When he is nervous and anxious, he eats to satisfy himself. Finally he develops all sorts of undesirable routines and lifestyles and it becomes impossible to restore him to normal way of living and normal health.

**Yoga is the solution to obesity.**

The Yogic method of dealing with obesity primarily involves two factors:

1. having food of a balanced and proper diet,

2. daily practice of selected postures (Asanas).

By practicing this yogic method, the individual does not have to go on fasting and one does not feel any weakness. The reduction in weight is so gradual that one does not feel any loss of strength or energy, and the reduction of weight and body conditioning occurs simultaneously.

Yoga practices need only fifteen to twenty minutes of your precious time daily. And it is recommended that once the weight has been reduced to normal level, one should keep practising Yoga even for a period of time as above mentioned daily and regularly. Finally, by taking a proper and balanced food, the normal weight will always stay the same.

**Selected Asanas, Postures:-**

These Asanas are very simple and easy to practise and they have enormous impact on weight reduction and body conditioning. One should not do too many Asanas in the start. One should proceed gradually but regularly and daily, mainly in the morning.

Now start with postures recommended for the first week and carry on adding postures of the second, third and other weeks, four, five and sixth weeks. A list of about twelve postures which are really easy can be performed by any one.

First Week

For the first week first, practise these few postures:-

1.  Ekpada Uttan Asana:– Four round with each legs a total of eight rounds.

2.  Uttanpada Asana:- Make a total of only for rounds daily and not more than six rounds.

3.  Rest posture:- Shavasana for at least five minutes after the postures are been executed.

Second week:- Continue to practise the two asanas and just add these below asanas.

4. Bhujanga Asana – Four rounds daily.

5. Salabha Asana – Four rounds daily as well.

After these continue the Shavasa Asana again for five minutes.

Third week:- After practicing the above four asanas, add again these below two asanas.

6. Sautulan Asanas – Do six rounds daily doing with each side alternately.

7. Pawanmukta Asana – about 3 rounds of each side alternately.

If possible, do this posture with both legs at the same time.

After follow with Shavasana for seven minutes.

Week Four:- keep performing all the above asanas and add these two postures more

8. Suryanamaskar Asanas the simple one, do four rounds.

9. Dhanur Asana:- Make 3 to 4 rounds. After these postures carry Shavasana for eight minutes.

Fifth week:- Continue all the above and add the two below.

10. Ardhavakra Asana: two with each side that is four rounds.

11. Paschimottan Asana – Make 3 to 4 rounds.

Carry with Shavasana for 10 minutes. Sixth week and continue always. Add these last two as well.

12. Supta Vajra Asana – Four rounds only.

13. Matsyendra Asana: Four rounds two round on each side.

**A diet to be followed : or you can make your own.**

Breakfast:-

1. Fruit juice – one cup of juice of any fruit, as orange, apple or pineapple etc..

2. Fresh fruit – one guava, banana, two peaches, an apple etc…

3. Or Germinated grain – ¼ cup soak from last night in water.

4. Wheat bread or toast – few pieces or cornflakes, oatmeal, wheat dalia with milk and brown sugar.

5. Eggs if desired one boiled, poached or scrambled.

6. Tea or coffee one cup (if desired)

Lunch and Dinner 12 to 1 p.m and 6 to 8 p.m.

1. Salad a mixture of tomato, cucumber, radish, lettuce, carrot etc with salt, pepper and lemon juice or with little salad dressing about a cup.

2. Soup of any type - one cup

3. Rice, bread or chapathi

4. Leafty vegetables of any kind.

5. Green veg of any kind.

6. Pulse like moong, masur, chana or lentil or any kind.

Afternoon Refreshment 4 to 5 p.m.

1. Fresh fruit of any type – one or two pieces

2. Salted biscuits a few pieces or dry fruits mixture of cashew, almond, pecan, pistachio and walnuts ¼ Cup.

3. Tea or coffee one cup only if needed.

N.B. If one is non-veg, he can take fish or liver or any sea food. He should avoid meat and chicken as far as possible. This diet would help in solving this obese problem, this chart becomes successful and important when the following principles, method and requirements are observed regularly and sincerely.

## N.B. OBESITY

Have two oranges everyday and plenty of water at least 8 glasses. Finally have 20 to 30 minutes of walking as a leisure time everyday if possible or at least 5 day weeks.

# CHAPTER 9

# ASANAS + PRANAYAMAS ON SPINAL PAIN AND BACK PAIN

Our spinal column is the most important frame of the body; without it, the body would not stand straight; it is the pillar of the whole body. Spinal pain is a problem mainly in the waist region. This pain could spread over both sides of the waist and the hips. When the pain is severe, the patient becomes almost invalid, unable to make any movement or any free physical movement. The sufferer could be bed-ridden for short or long term.

It is found that people carrying heavy weight's develop spinal pain as they grow older. Actually, with the stress and pressure of modern lifestyle, even young people are suffering from this spinal pain. The lower backache, at the initial stage might be tolerable and the individual might be able to bear it for some time; if prolonged, however, the pain becomes chronic and could eventually get aggravated.

The cause and healing:-

Actually there are four reasons for the spinal problems:

1. Wrong ways of eating and the resulting into overweight or underweight condition of the body.

2. Stay too long in cold.

3. Physical straining of the spine.

4. Bad sitting posture for some considerable length of time, mainly with moderate way of living involving those in sedentary occupations.

And it happens with the malformation of the spinal bones and columns as well.

Research has been found that large number of people suffering from this pain are in the constant habit of drinking water or tea or both after getting up in the morning. There are people who first drink water and then drink hot tea or coffee when they rise in the morning. This habit leads to force elimination of bowels, which in turn weakens the digestive system. So this empty condition of stomach affects the condition of the spinal, specially when the individual takes a bath or is exposed to the cold for a longer period. Excessive weight might be another cause for straining the spine. It might also be due to some sudden physical strain or to habitually defective ways of sitting of our modern time.

It has been found that by Yogic methods, the spinal pain is fully cured. If the pain is there longer, it might take longer to get cured. If it is then for a short time it might get cured in short days of practise.

The treatment implies taking the correct diet, sleeping on not too soft a bed and practising some selected Yoga postures given below. Tea and coffee and water while getting up should be stopped for a few months. Bananas and curd (dahi) should also be avoided for a period of time. Eating fatty, spicy and fried food should also be abstained from. Please do follow a correct diet and the advice on Chapter I of this book.

First Week Yogic Asanas.

Practice these Yoga postures

1. Pawan -Mukta Asana. Makarasana.

2. Bhujanga Asana. Rocking and rolling.

3. Shalabha Asana.

4. Ultanpada Asana.

5. Shava Asana – for 3 to 5 minutes.

Second Week

1. Pawan Mukta Asana – lying posture.

2. Bhujanga Asana – without any strain.

3. Salabha Asana – with one leg or two after

4. Ultanpada Asana – with one leg and with two legs after.

5. Ekpada Uttan Asana.

6. Rechaka – Puraka Pranayama.

7. Shavasana Asana – 5 to 7 minutes.

With these recommendations on diet and daily practise of Yoga postures, one will surely be cured of most pains and disorders in the spinal region without medical treatment.

2. Neck Pain

The causes of neck pain are many. It can be due to using of a very high pillow under the head while sleeping. Sometimes the head is being kept bending in a particular posture for long hours instead of remaining erect. It could be due to rigidity of the muscles and nerves in the neck and shoulders area which prevent the proper circulation of blood.

Here for the neck treatment, these are important.

1. Consuming a proper diet.

2. Remedying the faulty habits.

3. Practising some selected Yoga asanas, mainly for neck.

Neck exercises:-

Sit on the floor or in a chair keeping spine straight and eyes closed.

1. Throw the head lifelessly backwards and forwards in a slow motion.

2. Turn the head sideways to right and to the left.

3. Rotate the head clockwise.

4. Rotate the head counterclockwise, or anti-clockwise.

Repeat each exercise four to six times. Finish by patting the neck and back with your hands.

# CHAPTER 10

# DIABETES

Diabetes can be cured by Yoga postures. This is an ancient disease and nowadays millions and millions of people are suffering from this illness throughout the world. The symptoms of the disease are various but the cause of it is the excessive sugar in the blood and its passing out with the urine of the sufferers. The excessive accumulation of sugar in the blood is the source and is caused by the malfunctioning of the gland of pancreas.

It is a gland which is situated in the upper abdomen and if this does not produce enough insulin, finally the body fails to utilize the sugar and create energy from it. When sugar is not used properly by the gland, the body gets disturbed and the person starts to develop various physical ailments and disturbances. There is frequency of urination, excessive tiredness, loss of weight, blurring of the vision, general weakness and skin disorders in the sufferers. When the disease is chronic, hypertension (high blood pressure) and kidney disorders can be developed. Actually the method of treating this disease of diabetes is to inject insulin to replace the sugar which could not be produced by the pancreas. With this scientific treatment, the patient has to use it throughout his whole life and still can't eliminate it.

**Yoga aspects which can eliminate this diseases are:-**

1. proper diet

2. Regular practice of Yoga postures; by practising these Yoga postures regularly, the disease can be cured within a period of two to three months.

These Yogic asanas (postures) can restore the normal functioning of the pancreas and other glands of the endocrinal system. It is clear that when these glands begin to work properly, the body chemistry becomes normal, and the sufferer is fully recovered from his diabetic problems and his health is restored to a normal level. This is the miraculous factor of Yoga practises in daily life.

Some asanas to make those glands to normality. There is a selected asanas which can help to revive the normal functioning of the endoctrinal system.

And there are some easier postures which can be practised by everyone.

They are:

1. Surya namaskara.

2. Uttan pada Asana.

3. Bhujanga Asana.

4. Shalabha Asana.

5. Paschimottan Aasana.

6. Ardha Vakra Asana.

7. Matsyendra Asana.

8. Supta Vajra Asana.

9. Dhanur Asana.

10. Shavasana.

Out of these above only six to seven of those asanas can cure diabetes. But practice is essential not theory. PRACTICE MAKES PERFECT. Always Remember.

# CHAPTER 11

# EYE PROBLEMS

Here, certain Yogic measures are introduced to cure some eye defects concerned mainly with the power of the eye vision. However, the Yogic steps of cure are not applied for correcting the organic defects like cataract, glaucoma and other disorders of this nature and which have already been in a state of chronic situation. In these cases, the defects should be treated by eyes specialists, whereas in cases where surgical treatment is not useful, disorders like eye strains, eye pain, diminishing of visionary power, near and far sightedness and other vision problems can be cured through the yogic treatment. The treatments which do not require any surgery and are liable to be cured by medicinal helps, can be treated through Yoga without any medicines. Actually visionary eye disorders are alarming problem throughout the world. The cause for this visionary disorder is mainly the cause of malnutrition. It is crystal clear that millions and millions of people cannot afford to have a proper diet and that which affects the health and wholly the vision power also is getting affected, and their eyes gradually get weaker and weaker. If everything seems normal but one still becomes a victim of eye disorder of non organic type, this is due to the faulty eating and some undesirable habits. Many have the habits of eating mostly fried, highly spicy and mix seasoned food. Others have the habit of drinking too much coffee and tea or hard liquor, smoking too much, lack of sleep with undue straining of the eyes. There are 3 types of these eye sufferers.

1. Bad habits of eating mainly those who cannot afford a balanced diet and this causes malnutrition .

2. Some who can afford but are in the habit of eating only a particular type of food which can also cause malnutrition; (In French: on mange bien mais mal).

3. Others who suffer from certain identified undesirable habits.

The above patient who is suffering from one of these 3 types can cure his eye-problems with only a little care and attention.

**Cure is possible**

The patients who suffer from these eye disorders need to have special care to their diet and correcting certain bad dietary habits. They must discontinue to eat things which are harmful to the vision of their eyes and must consume food that is conducive to the growth and restoration of the visionary power.

**Some Asanas to protect the eyes:-**

1. Suryanamaskar Asana.

2. Trikonaasana.

3. Bhujanga Asana.

4. Yoga Mudra.

5. Jalandhar Bandha.

6. Shavasana.

7. Some Eyes Exercises.

**Some Eyes Exercises:-**

This should be practised after Shavasana. They are of two types. A and B.

**A Eye Exercise:-**

The movements should be done only with the eyes and without any movement of head or neck. The head, neck and spine should be erect, only move the eyes as directed. Don't strain the eye which is very important. Now proceed on:

1. Sit in Sukhasna posture. Keep the spine, neck and head straight on. Look infront at the level of the eyes. Breathe normally.

2. Move the eyes, upwards towards the sky or ceiling, stay there for two seconds. Then look downward towards the earth and stay there for two seconds. Again look towards the sky and after staying there for two seconds, look downwards and stay there for two seconds. Do this upwards and downward movement twice. This makes one unit of the exercise. After close the eyes for two seconds.

3. Then open the eyes and look in front. Now look towards the right side and try to see as far as you can. Then look towards the left side and stay there for two seconds and try to see as far as possible. Then look again to the right side. Then go to the left side. Now look in front again. Close your eyes. Once this left and right exercise is over, finally keep the eyes closed for six to eight seconds.

Remember that one unit of up-down movement plus one unit of right - left movement connected are counted as one round of this eye exercise. When one round is over, rest for six to eight seconds. After resting for

168

a few seconds, make two more rounds of this up-down and left-right exercise. As one practises this exercise, one unconsciously learns how to practise eye movements systematically.

One should do them daily. During first week, do two rounds daily. Second week onwards, do three to four rounds daily. After performing them, do the palming exercise.

**The Palming exercise:-**

Put the palms against each other so that heat is generated in the palms by this function. After rubbing the palms for eight to ten seconds place the left palm on the left eye and the right palm on the right eye, no pressure should be felt on the eyes. Keep them on the eyes till the palms get cold. One can do two rounds of palming.

**B. exercise of the eye:-**

In this exercise, the eyes should move clockwise and anticlock-wise motion. When the movement is done according to the movement of the arms of the clock, it is called clockwise and when the movement is reversed it is called anticlock-wise.

**These are the steps of B eyes exercises:-**

1. Look straight infront, lift the eyes up and start, moving them in a circular way coming to the right side and then go down, then to the left side and then upward again. This is one round of this clockwise exercise. Repeat this twice and rest for six to eight second and keep the eyes closed.

2. Now the anticlock-wise movement of the eyes. Look in front of the eyes. Then look upward towards the ceiling, then to the left side, then down, then come to the right side, then upward

again in a circular way. This is one anticlock-wise movement of the eyes. Do this movement twice. This makes one round of anticlock-wise movement. Rest for six and eight seconds. Keep the eyes closed.

One unit of clockwise and one of anticlock-wise exercise make round of B exercise. Do this clockwise and anticlockwise exercise for two rounds and rest for ten seconds eyes closing. After resting, do the palming for three to four times. After this palming the exercise is over.

From the second week onward, first practise four rounds of group A. The four rounds group B. After complete the practice of A&B, do four rounds of palming in the end. One can either do only one session in the morning or one can do the same in the evening. And one can do only the eye exercises without doing Yoga.

The chart of diet is annexed to obesity chapter, one can follow the same diet. A proper diet, that is the followers should not eat fatty, fried, roasted and hard to digest eatable. They should stop taking meat, chicken highly seasoned or spicy food. They should avoid eating pickles, red pepper and other items which strain the nervous system. They should give up tea, coffee and smoking.

# CHAPTER 12

# CONCLUSION

One must follow two examples and actions: be like the 1. the salmon fish in the river, which always swims against the current. 2. Like the Lotus flower which comes out of the dirty pond, but never carries away dirt while blossoming.

## The way to Happiness

To reach happiness is an inborn, deep-rooted and natural desire of all human beings. Man does everything for the sake of happiness. A human being is never satisfied until he reached complete happiness with fulfilment that includes perfect peace, love, wisdom, joy and bliss. After all, all our inner self is filled with love, peace and happiness but which are dormant. The closer one reaches into the inner self or real self, the more happiness, joy and peace one experiences.

However, it is very strange and cynical to see how humanity is baffled and searched for this happiness in material things related to the world, in possessions of wealth, woman and wine, the three W's in outer conditions which are unreal and finally in relationships with other persons, such as friends, relatives and mainly in hot pursuit of money and the dubs into a money-wise situation to gratify their material needs. Such worldly and material pursuits have never been fully gratified and which will never till the end comes in this finite world. "Humans are always seeking it in the wrong place, so they are gradually losing touch with it" goes a saying.

Most people are wasting their precious time searching for happiness at the wrong place, outwardly; eventually that brings desperation and deception. Finally, they experience tremendous resentment and anger, jealousy; ego-centeredness and hatred accumulating in the process which leads to a lot of violence, very often in their lives.

The truth is that happiness is within all of us and to reach it, one needs to turn within his inner world and travel toward his innerself, which is the fountain of infinite Bliss and Peace and one can bath from it as much as one wants. It is achieved, only when one practises Yoga and meditation which are the paths leading one to his inner journey towards the real self-consciousness, with purity of mind and full control of the greatest enemy of man, the five senses. This is the only way, even if one wants to live in this material world. But it is not easy but is possible by acquiring a strong body by practising Asanas for the body and Pranayama and food disciplines for the brain and mind. My spiritual advice is that Ayurvedic, Yoga as a Science and the quality vegetarian foods should be adopted in everyone's life in order to remain disease free.

In this world, it is impossible to find perfect and true happiness in anything or anyone and in any situation. This unreal or material world is changeable and destructible within any second. It is very logical to understand that temporary things and situation cannot bring one lasting and permanent joy. In this state of constant flux, we can only experience that which brings temporary and illusory sensation and contentment. It is also crystal clear that one has to comprehend that creation is built on the principle of duality; if one is born, one must die.

In this nature of duality, everything is made of two opposite sides, like of a coin. These two opposite sides can't be separated from each other and there is the inbuilt of the Law of nature since immemorial creation.

The inference is that anything which brings pleasure also brings pain. And anything or person that is associated, must also be dissociated and left at anytime or some time. All advantages have their disadvantages in this unreal material world, either one believes it or not. There is a saying which says that what appears is not always real.

Remember carefully that there is the Law of Divinity and balance. If one wants to avoid pains and discomforts in this life, one will have to avoid comforts and pleasures as well.

If one doesn't want to be insulted, one will have to give up the pleasure of praising as well.

Most people crave after only the good things in this material life, but this is impossible. Such misconception is only man's biggest trap in this world. In this dualistic material world, one can't just have one side of the coin without the other. "The basic principle is that what one craves at the inner level of one's being can't be found in anything of this illusion world." goes a saying.

If one wants to acquire real joy and bliss, one will have to transcend this duality of this material world. Bear in mind that the only way to remain unaffected by this dual law of nature of this world is to face this duality of worldly things or incidents with a detached and discriminated outlook as if one is merely a spectator or a witness; which means that one should neither get exhilarated in success nor get disillusioned in loss or failure. My advice to anyone is to try to stay very often even-minded in the face of duality, either in success or loss etc, etc.

If one could reach this mental height, one could become free from the grips of the world dualities.

There is also one motive why no one gets satisfied in what one wants, because one always wants more and more no matter what one gets the worldly things are all related to each other. It is true that whatever one gets, there is always better things available and one starts looking towards them and in this manner, one always stays dissatisfied and discontented, no matter what one gets. Finally, there is nothing pure, perfect or absolute or complete in the nature of the world of relativity.

Remember that the origin of Bliss is the Innerself. This Bliss or everlasting joy is very free from any opposite effects and which resides inside oneself, which is the innerself, within everyone on this earth and which is as well the deep recesses of the inner-most core, call it what you like (soul, consciousness) etc, etc. This is the highest goal which all of us should struggle to find through the practices of the Science of Yoga.

It is obvious that as one becomes more aware of one's inner self through the Science of Yoga, one will definitely withdraw from dependence on objects and people as sources of contentment or gratification. But that doesn't mean that one will no longer enjoy outside experiences. In fact, one will enjoy this world more, being more non-attached, free without any expectations from it. However, this means that one will not depend on the world for one's satisfaction, comfort and stability; one's satisfaction and contentment will rest within oneself. When one is dependent on people and objects for one's pleasure, then one's whole vision gets blurred. One is then not able to relate to them freely and with joy. Remember that seeking happiness in the illusion world leads to small momentary islands of satisfaction in the midst of a preponderance of restlessness.

People have false beliefs and illusions, imagining that for their happiness, someone or something external to them must have a change. Very often, no one or situations around them can be changed. No one can change and regulate this world as none is the controller of this material world. One must try one's level best to change oneself; on the contrary, one should focus more in the Inner change, in the mental attitudes and reactionary patterns based on right living and knowledge, of wisdom and the path of spirituality. One should definitely try to change and improve one's outside environment by making it more positive, harmonious and pleasant. One should also practise to control mind and thought and reponses inorder that nothing can disturb one, no matter what occurs from the outside world.

Such external actions are never as important as the reactions towards them. However difficult the external realities and facts may be, it is the mental attitude towards them which matters more.

The external actions only act as a fuel which can catch fire only when it is lighted by the matchstick of the mind.

Remember these words, mind, senses, intellect, body and self-complex.:

1. Body stands for chariot,

2. senses are the horses.

3. Mind is the reins.

4. Intellect is the driver.

5. The Self who dwells within is the Lord of the chariot.

"Unless the horses are well controlled and the reins firmly held, unless the driver is intelligent, the chariot may be thrown into the ditch and get crashed. However, if the discriminative faculty is used, that is if the driver follows the path of right thinking, then he has perfect control on both horses and chariot is the teaching of the Bhagavad Gita.

Most of people's mind is not able to stay quiet even for a moment. The mind is always after something materially. People make their minds filled with deep-rooted habits and a type of mind-set.

Even when there is nothing to worry about, people search some cause for worry and stay under free floating anxiety. If there is nothing to do, they are still more tense as to what to do now, instead of utilizing this opportunity to relax or concentrate their minds by applying the path of the Science of Yoga.

In Yoga, one learns how to reduce the velocity of the mind, that is how to slow down one's mind essentially, which means reducing the number of thoughts in the mind. For example, one thousand thoughts rush across one's mind at the same time; now try to make only hundred thoughts to move at the same time. That means that one has to calm down the mind to that extent. Remember that the velocity of mind is really high during emotions of hurry, impatience and desperation. This shows that the mind is weak and uncontrolled at that extent. One should remain in the present and learn how to live in the present. Don't remain in the past and anticipate or apprehend the future. To remain as most of us do, the mind becomes very poor and weak in any performance of the daily actions or works.

Boredom and loneliness have no place in a spiritual path. They only exist among ordinary and common way of living of people of this material world. Very often lonely person can't face himself and this man runs after other objects and people, friends and relatives to keep his mind occupied daily. When people do not have any object or person to engage their minds, they are bored. Boredom comes from wanting to get something but not having it. They do not realize that joy can also be gained without objects by turning the attention within themselves, by practising the path of Yoga. By relying on other persons, friends, relatives and objects for self satisfaction is really illusory, for none is going to stay permanently with anyone in this material world. The time when everything will leave anyone is that time when one has to live only within oneself.

"If anyone can't live alone, that means he is not at peace within himself," is a wise dictum. There are many conflicts and disturbances inside him which begin to trouble him as soon as he sits alone. In order to escape them, one always wants some external things, objects and persons, friends, relatives so that one's mind may stay preoccupied in outward material things instead of his internal peace. One uses these tricks as a scape-goat, but it won't stop and won't give one the eternal peace and comfort which one is caring for at the centre of his heart. Sooner or later, one has to come to the core of oneself to get the peace one is looking for. The fact is that running away from oneself is never the root to attain bliss or joy. The only and main practice is that one has to learn to dive within, to live within one innerself. People have all created it as a habit to live in crowd. They are afraid to be alone, even though the reality is that their loneliness is their true and worthy companion

Remember these words; "One has come in this world alone, one is alone and one will depart alone."

Man should recognize his loneliness, that is he must experience it and feel or know it. One should for a short time live as though he is alone in this world. During that precious solitude, forget all, either a husband, or a wife, a father, an officer or a student, or a man or a woman. One is just the truth of oneself and try to reach that image that he is one with the Divinity, God.

People's minds are very biased and vague and narrow. They think that the way to one's development and happiness is to accumulate as many things and objects as possible, encounter as many people, friends and relationships in life as possible, change many jobs as far as possible, travel to many places as possible etc, etc.. Unfortunately, life has shown that such people are the most dissatisfied group and finally when they are tired with their life and think back, they wonder what is all about and why have they submitted to all these wrong impulses?

In fact, the reality is that true joy is not in amassing things, but rather in giving up and "letting go". That is the more one lets go, the more satisfied and relaxed one becomes. The truth is that when one lets go of everything, one becomes completely free and detached. Be very careful when I mention "letting go". This does not mean throwing and leaving everything one has. One may have everything and still he may be mentally detached from it. This is called the true "letting go". "

"Be in the world, but not of the world," as the saying goes.

However, this "letting go" is not applicable only to material experiences; it also applies to various emotions rooted in the mind. An example here is given: Suppose one has some worries about something in the mind, that is jealously and hatred toward a person, just allow these feelings to drop as a stone falling in the river and let oneself be free.

In fact, there is always a strong discomfort in sticking to something when there is a feeling of relief and relaxation in letting-go the thing. If one gets attached or stuck to something, freedom of the thought and action is lost. Then one is likely to think and act in this material world in terms of these attachments. One won't be able to see Truth as it is. So the ignorance of reality creates discomfort and dissipation and stops one's further growth along the path of spirituality and true happiness.

Form a spiritual point of view, one who can conquer the Ego within can become Divine. The ego is a wall or veil which stands between human and God. If one dissolves the ego, one comes face to face with God.

From Yoga psychological point of view, the separation of 'I' from all means one's feeling of detachment from worldly wrong bonds; there is only God and complete existence. Ego prevails when one wants to feel important, superior to others, where one wants to prove to others that "He is something;" in other words, ego is associated with the feeling of superiority, importance and pride within himself, due to possession of material things and objects.

Ego means "I and mine";. that is, the more the ego, the more narrow one's personality and consciousness becomes, and in this state one tends to view everything from a narrow angle and selfish ends not as it really is. That "I" "Me," "Mine" constitute the bondage of the individual. In order to have genuine liberation, one has to practise to be free from "NOT I, NOT MINE" Furthermore these two terms of "Not I not Mine," will give ultimate peace and bliss and nearly all problems come to the end. Finally the tribulations of the spirit and soul of the individual can be over. Owing to the ego, people don't reach God because they don't want to lose themselves from the possession of Egoness. And they don't want to become 'Nobody" but want to be somebody in this material and fake world which one has to leave here after in whatever situation in death. Why then get entangled in the circle of birth and death? But this feeling of "Nobody" spontaneously makes one "Every body," without any effort on one's part.

However, to be "Nobody" is not a state of emptiness or boredom as humans misinterpret it. It is on the contrary a state of bliss, joy and peace. When one practises the Science of Yoga, one realizes this purity of Iness or the pure consciousness. When someone goes deeper and deeper in this Yoga practice, he transforms himself. With this true awareness, one can remove all one's sufferings and delusion. In this transcendental awareness, one reaches the true and original nature or the inner-most consciousness.

The ego or false "I" is only a superimposition over the original nature and is not a permanent part of human and can be rejected as soon as one wakes up from the sleep of ignorance, hypocrisy, selfishness and the false character of the ego.

"Wise is he who by spiritual revelation recognises his own weakness and strength, ignorance, knowledge, frustration and sufficiency, a sage has said" Actually most people in this material world are full of hypocrisy, ignorance and selfishness (ego) habits. They do everything in their daily life in such above-mentioned habits. It is high time that each individual be self-equipped. He must begin to wake himself and accept some portions of elementary spiritual reality. One does not have to be in any special group, institution, creed, religion or any organization to practise spirituality. Neither does one need to leave whatever group organization or religion one belongs to. Such change is of no-importance; a good life leads to satisfaction, while a wrong one to suffering. If one can bring oneself to believe in a law of recompense and the existence of some divine power behind it and if one would make some effort to improve one's own character and unfold the innerself or resources, one will be armed and armoured his one defence in this illusory world.

With evolution, man has to liberate himself from former enslavements. He should start to seek in himself, in his own latent and wonderful resources the help he needs. This is the first step to the final one, to find divinity within himself, which after all is the ultimate and grand objective of his earthly incarnation.

Life becomes exclusively arbitrary, if man submits all his thinking, response and living upon others. He will eventually become too enervated or debilitated to think, respond and act on his own capacity. Then, he is unable to hold a thought unless he has received it from outside, then he cannnot make a single decision of his own, but has to run to others to make it for him. When and how can one grow? A person has to begin now to free himself from the racial suggestion imposed on him, has to start establishing by effort his creative attitude towards life. It is now high time for him to show, however vaguely, some of the attributes of maturity. He must cast aside passive unthinking acquiescence in false institutions and become more responsible for his own belief and his own life.

A life of simple tastes and independent of others tends to foster inner tranquillity. Only by becoming simple can man come back to a more natural way of living and consequently lead a more spiritual and healthier existence.

Psychology and Hinduism are not religions, but they only guide and teach Man to follow the Truth. One has to understand the Truth and then go into practice. These never coerce any one to do this or not to do that. You have to decide for your own self. An example: they never advise you not to eat or to eat meat, but they give you the clear details: reasons and explanations of what the meat is. It is up to you to decide either to eat or not to eat it. They all teach Man the way of right living through out their lives. The choice is yours; no one is to be blamed and God is innocent. You are your own destiny and fate.

It is all your own past Karma (action) of what you are today. Your future Karma (action) depends on what Karma (action) you are doing in your present time life.

Do bad, your Karma (action) = fruit is bad and sour. Do good, your Karma (action) = Fruit is good and sweet.

The truly spiritual man teaches others how to look at things, as they are in reality. Therefore, the greatest benefactor of the world is a true spiritual teacher, and not the man who selfishly gives million of dollars to help the poorer classes with clothes and food in return for a decoration.

Often the rich spare their money to the poorer only as a show off. And the intellectuals share their intelligence of the material, the scientist only to invent and aggravate the situation of the modern world with devilish inventions.

Many indulge in luxuries only to the body, to be in luxurious situation. But they are not uplifting their souls and the involution of human character. As soul is greater than the body, so the man who opens the spiritual eyes of any individual and makes him see things in their spiritual light is the greatest benefactor.

Unfortunately the mind of most people in this world is really very sick and contaminated with all sorts of illusions which cannot keep them still, and they cannot remain peaceful. Their mind is like the rough waves of the sea. The five senses often torture them through daily life, and they become the slaves of them.

Finally I have to thank all my surroundings, those who have helped my spiritual life, made me come nearer to my own Innerself. Even with my weak body since childhood, I have built up a very strong and firm mind with positive thoughts always to face many problems in whatever circumstances. I have learnt with awareness and love how to be like a lotus flower in this illusion world. This is really a gold mine which I have developed all the way long. I have to thank my inner and outside Guru for all those noble and spiritual Gyans (wisdom of knowledge) and I feel having experienced the highest goal of my life, the road of freedom to Divinity. Some may read this book and think that I am impressing myself with the Ego, but I only want to show you the reality of life after having attained the highest culmination in this human form. So I advise anyone first try to awaken his Inner Guru, who is dormant always and once this is done, then nothing on earth can prevent one from attaining this precious path of our spirituality and to meet his outer Guru.

I am quite aware how hard it is to be against this material life, but nothing is impossible if one is determined and have faith and pure love to face the deceptive powers and to transform them into a true and real divinity which is lying within all of us. One can turn the words Ego to positive living and by giving a positive meaning to each word. (Ego)

E = Exhibition, Expansion of the innerself.

G = Good which is God.

O = the Omniscient, Omnipotent and Omnipresent Lord.

Remove the 3 words " EGO" what remains on the exhibition or expansion of one's Inner Self, good which is God and love thy Lord who is Omniscient, Omniportent and Omnipresent.

Know thyself, then all will be clear and you will become free. We are all image of God as we all come from Him and without Him nothing exists at all.

N.B.: GEETA CHAP IX Verses: 20-21

"This word "SURENDRAHLOKAM" is a sacred word where only the Lord resides in. So I have been initiated by this name of SURENDRHANANDA. My duty is to take along with me all of those who devote, follow or are in touch with me, to the above world within this human form in whatever circumstances."

I must say that 99.999 of most human beings mind is being fragmented. They are rich in wealth, women, wine, attached to materially intellectual pursuits and full of egocentricism. I wish by the grace of Lord, they could change themselves and seek for Reality, the Innerself and seek Him within themselves through this only precious human birth. Then the truth will be revealed as their own right.

I am in Him, He is within me

"A man may have lived for five hundred years and if that time he has not reached the state of God-consciousness, he is little better than an oak tree which may outlast many generations and grow to great size, but is in the end only an oak tree. That man on the contrary, who dies at the age of thirty, having realized his Oneness with Divinity, has achieved Infinite more than he who possesses perfect health, longevity, psychic powers, or the gift of healing, for he has become a living God in this world and can point the way of salvation to all mankind."

The reality is that Divinity can't be found in books or scriptures; one must do the daily practice of Yoga – (Sadhana Spiritual discipline and Practice) individually and with devotion, love, purity, will-power, faith, detachment and discrimination and finally must be neutral or indifferently spiritually.

Once the Ajna Chakra (the Third Eye) is opened, then one is sure to be on the true road to Divinity in this only human form.

*A true religion is a complete practical subject in one's life. It is based wholly upon practice regularly and daily, but does not base upon theory or speculation of any sort, for religion begins only when theory stops.*

To open the Ajna Chakra (Third eye) the following steps below are needed:-

1. Yoga – to practice daily.

2. Food – Discipline very important.

3. Breathing & Postures – should be maintained.

4. Guru – Spiritual Master is the gateway to God.

5. Character of a Lotus Flower, must be example to practise daily.

Spirituality never depends on the reading or studying of scriptures, or upon learned interpretation of Sacred Books, or upon fine theological arguments, but upon the realization of unchangeable TRUTH.

Infact, a man is called really Spiritual or Religious not because he has written some books, nor because he has the gift of oratory and can express eloquent sermons, or be a Philosopher, a Psychologist, or a learned intellectually, but because he expresses divine powers through his words, deeds and actions. Remember that a thoroughly illiterate person can reach the highest state of spiritual perfection without going to any school or university, and without reading any scripture, only if he can be able to conquer his animal natures by realizing his true Self and his relation to the Universal Spirit, or if he can be able to attain the wisdom Knowledge of that TRUTH which dwells or develops within him, and which is the same as the Infinite Source of Existence, Intelligence and Bliss.

It is also crystal clear that our worst evil is the Ego that binds us to this material world, and prevents us from attaining that highest path of realization. We live a wrong way by assuming that we are the limited Ego, tyrannized by an equipment body, mind (brain) intellect complex, shamelessly struggling to increase our happiness from the world outside with false objects, emotions and thoughts. We have for so long lived with such a false idea and character that no amount of study and reflection can erase our tendency or impression.

However, he who has mastered all the scriptures, philosophies and sciences may be considered by this modern society as an intellectual phenomenon, but still he cannot be equal to that illiterate character who having been able to realize this eternal Reality has become one with Him, who sees God everywhere, and who lives on earth as an embodiment of Divinity. He is the spiritual man whose spiritual eye (Third Eye) has opened. These spiritual powers begin to manifest in the soul that is awakened.

Whatever one calls it, spiritual eye, Third Eye, sixth sense or Ajna Chakra, it is found between the eye brow in the middle. This spiritual eye is within each one of us, but it is opened in very few only among millions, and they are known as true Yogis.

In the vast majority of beings, it is underdeveloped or at primary state, coated by a dark veil. It is clear and true that through the practice of

Yoga, it unfolds in man who becomes conscious of the higher invisible realms and of everything that exists on the Soul plane.

Bear in mind that senses cannot lead beyond the superficial appearance of sense objects. We invent instruments after instruments, but these instruments again have their ends. Thus the struggle goes on more and more, discovering at each step how poor and helpless are our sense powers in relation to the Knowledge of Wisdom. Veils after veils may be rent asunder, but still veils after veils will stay behind. "Innumerable are the branches of knowledge, but short is our time and many are the obstacles in the path. So the Yogis and Wise men should first struggle to know that which is the highest truth. And of all the knowledge which is the highest truth, this has been the concluded answer i.e "Know Thyself"

"If thou can learn the true nature of thine own Self, thou wilt know the reality of the Universe."

"In thy true self thou wilt find the Eternal Truth, the Infinite Source of all phenomena. Finally by knowing this, thou wilt know God and His whole creation."

These above citations are precious; follow them.

One should stick to one's duty first to acquire this Self Knowledge before one tries to know anything concerning the objects of sense-perception. No one can get it through books or the study of external phenomena, but by studying our own nature, and by practising the several branches of Yoga, through a Guru (Spiritual Master).

Finally it is better that each one becomes his own doctor within this daily life. Meanwhile get time to scrutinize one's own Innerself and judge one's own self. Never worry and get stress about world affairs and family affairs. They are the real tortures and mind-shattering in daily life.

AUM - AMEN - AMIN

# CHAPTER 13

# Some Spiritual and Yoga Thoughts

1. When one becomes the controller of mind and thoughts, that is a master, nothing bad and good can affect it. One is no more the slave of this material world; one becomes free from the bondage of anything in this only world. This world is a paradise and he, the genuine spiritual man, is the king of kings.

2. Someone can change only himself in his entire life span but can't change anybody else.

3. If anyone surrenders himself to God, there is no limit to what he can achieve.

4. Truth will always stay Truth, even if there is not a single follower of It.

5. Spirituality doesn't mean non-possession of things. It only means non-attachment. A king possessing enormous wealth may be totally unattached while a beggar with torn clothes may be a highly attached person.

6. The greatest man is he who is a servant of all.

7. The Ego is the greatest barrier between you and God. It acts like a wall between you and God. Once this ego is dissolved, you come face to face with God.

8. Spirituality doesn't mean leaving the world and actions and going into retirement. It only means a change of mental attitude while doing the same karmas (good actions) and living in the same world.

9. The best way to keep yourself happy is to ensure that others are happy too.

10. Nobody can exercise any power upon you unless you give them the opportunity to do so.

11. The greatest fear to man in the world comes from himself only and not from any outside source.

12. Nothing in this universe can affect or frighten you, unless your mind allows itself to be affected. Such is the power of mind.

13. Mind is your greatest friend as well as your biggest enemy. If you use it properly, it is your best friend, if you misuse it, it is your greatest enemy.

14. One ounce of practice is better than ten tons of theory.

15. Real preaching is through correct behaviour and conduct, not by words.

16. A joyous spirit will always find reasons to be happy in any circumstances.

17. A gloomy spirit will always find reasons to be unhappy in any circumstances.

18. The fears which we experience in the outside world come from our inside only, although it doesn't appear to be so. By deep

contemplation, you may realize that you yourself are the source of your fears.

19. Sickness is more in the mind than in the body. You can't be sick until you feel sick.

20. Anger, provocation, irritation only shows that instead of being the master, we are still the slaves of our lower mind (the animal mind or automatic mind).

21. One must accept all sufferings and miseries in life; then they will leave you more easily and hastily.

22. True spirituality transcends all religions.

23. Money can give you everything material except happiness. It has the power to make you miserable in comforts.

24. Wise men learn from fools more than what fools learn from them.

25. The person who is same in thought, word and deed is only fit to be a realized soul.

26. The purpose of spiritual development is to rise above the limitations of mundane living.

27. The person who has controlled his mind has almost attained God.

28. For a true spiritual seeker, there is nothing which is low or high, trivial or important. Everything and every occasion is an opportunity for him in the path of liberation.

29. When you are able to overcome worldly pleasures and pains, attractions and repulsion, you don't experience simply a blank or void; you experience a spiritual awakening in yourself.

30. The more one involves in worldly pleasures and enjoyments, the more one gets bound and entangled and the more difficult it becomes for one to be free from them and get liberated.

31. A person who is stabilized in soul consciousness and God consciousness, considers all worldly things and objects of pleasure like garbage. For him, there is no difference between gold and stone.

32. A child always remains tension free. Similarly one can also be tension free if one considers oneself as the child of divinity.

# Either

# YOGA CHART FOR ASANAS POSTURES

1. Guru, Master Prayer

2. Suryanamaskar (Asana 12 Postures – before starting)

3. Yoga Nidar – Concentration either on tip, front of nose or eyes brow.

4. Rocking and Rolling

5. Pawan

6. Ultanapadasau

7. Ardhahalasan

8. Halasana

9. Paschimotlanasana

10. Konasana

11. Bhujangasana

12. Shalabhasana

13. Dhanurasana

14. Makarasana

15. Ardhamatsyendrasana

16. Vajrasana

17. Sarvangasana

18. Matsyasana

19. Shirshasana

20. Tadasana

21. Shavasana

22. Trataka (Concentration on any diety or postures of Candle)


Ending with Peace, Peace, Peace.

**OR**

## YOGA CHART FOR PRANAYAMAS (Breathing Exercises)

1. Guru, Master Prayer

2. Suryanamaskar – (Asanas 12 Postures) before starting.

3. Yoga Nidra

4. Bastrika

5. Kapalbhati

6. Bahya Pranayama

7. Nauli in Sitting Position

8. Anuloma Viloma

9. Bhramari

10. Shitari

11. Sitkari

12. Suryabhedi

13. Chandrabhedi

14. Omkar – Either on 7 Chakras or just concentration on Ajnachakra

15. Simhasina

16. Shavasana – dead corpse relaxation

## 17. Concentration (TRATAKA)

Ending with Peace, Peace, Peace.

# YOGA CHART

## FOR CHILDREN AND ADULT AND OLD AGE

*But a master is greatly needed, not advice from Cassette or Books*
*for Either or Both Pranayama and Asana*

## PRANAYAMA

Bhastrika

Kapalbhati

Bahya

Anuloma Viloma

Bhramari

Om 7 times

Ujjyagi

Shitali or Sitkari

Simhasina (lion posture)


**ASANA Main Postures**

Siddhasana or Sukhasana

Sirshasana

Sarvahgasana

Mat Syana

Padan gushthasana

Ardha Matsyendrasana

Dhanushrasana

Vigrasana

Shavasana. Relaxation

Concentration – Trataka


Om Shanti, Shanti, Shanti